15 Minutes to a Great Puppy

Kevin Michalowski

Published by

700 East State Street • Iola, WI 54990-0001
715-445-2214 • 888-457-2873

Our toll-free number to place an order or obtain
a free catalog is (800) 258-0929.

Library of Congress Catalog Number: 2004113664

ISBN 13-digit: 978-0-87349-917-0
ISBN 10-digit: 0-87349-917-4

Designed by Kara Grundman
Edited by Don Gulbrandsen

Printed in Canada

Dedication

To my boys, Adam and Ethan. May you both find as much joy in life as you have brought me.

Acknowledgments

My wife has put up with my dogs and my writing for more than a decade now. She deserves some credit. Also, special thanks to all those people who gave of their time and talent to help make this book great: M.D. and Julie, Mark, Sandi, Kevin Howard, Dr. Arleigh Reynolds and all the folks at Purina and all the rest who added their two cents' worth. This book is only possible because I had help. If I've missed anyone, I'm sorry.

Table of Contents

Introduction

It's only a puppy. How much trouble can it be?

That's the kind of line you'd hear in a low-budget horror film — just before the cute little guy cuts loose with a deafening roar and devours half the senior class.

But you can avoid this kind of carnage. You can control the puppy, any puppy, with just the power of your mind. You can housebreak your pup, control its incessant barking, and make the puppy come, sit, lie down and fetch on command all by investing just a few quality minutes in your new pet. With just a couple of short training sessions each day you will soon have a puppy of which you can be proud—one that will grow into a fine dog and a lifelong companion. All you have to do is focus your training and care during those critical first few months of the puppy's life.

Kids and dogs are a great combination.

Puppy trouble starts early. Most of the time you don't even notice that you're making mistakes until you are faced with bad behavior on the part of your dog. To put a more positive spin on things, it is also true that puppy greatness also starts early. If you are: firm, but gentle; patient, but persistent; and, above all, consistent and kind, you have all the basics for creating a great puppy. Which leads me to another important point: good puppies and great dogs are made, not born. The breeding gives you a healthy dog — that's about it. If you take the best puppy with the most distinguished pedigree from a long line of champions or field champions and mess up the training, all that good breeding and all that money you spent will be wasted. On the other hand, a refugee from the pound helped along with patient and effective care and training can end up as the greatest dog you've ever owned. Good puppies are all about how you act and react. You have all the power. Use it wisely.

With this book it is my hope to teach you that you can develop a great puppy quickly and easily, without abandoning all other aspects of your life. Follow the training and care instructions presented here and you'll reduce your stress level, be happier about owning a puppy and generally have a happier, healthier dog. If you have 15 minutes to invest each day, you, too, can have a great puppy.

Kevin Michalowski
August 2004

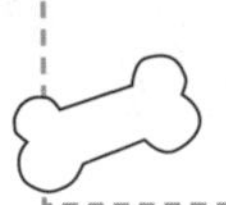

Good puppies and great dogs are made, not born.

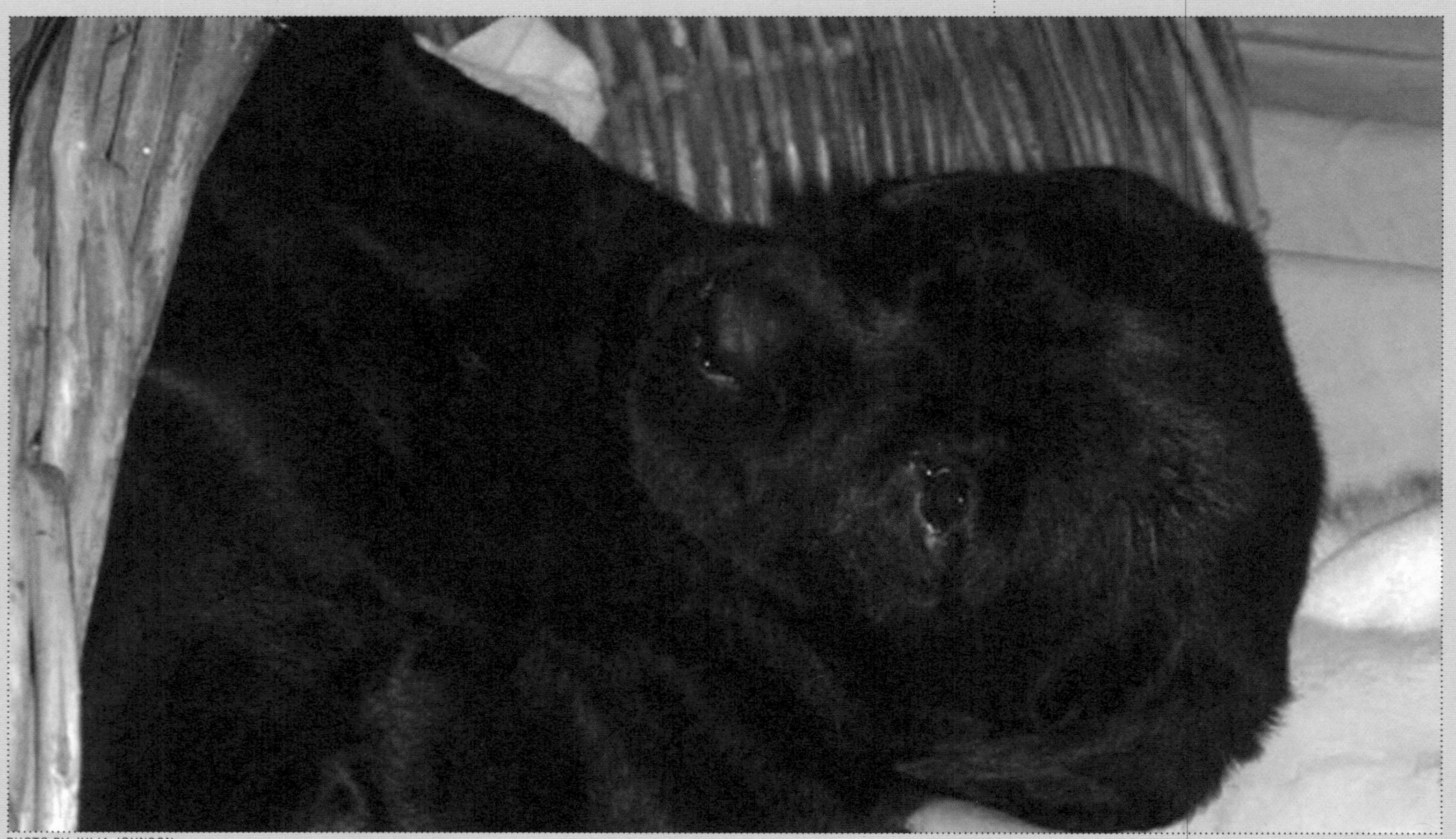

PHOTO BY JULIA JOHNSON

Chapter One

The Pre-Puppy Checklist

The list of things you need before you get a puppy does not just cover the implements needed for puppy care and training. Choosing to own a puppy is almost a question of philosophy. You can have everything you need, but still not have everything you need. It's about attitude as much as it is about hardware. Sometimes you don't find that out until after you have all the hardware.

Choosing a puppy means choosing a long-term companion. It's a big commitment, but it's not overwhelming.

What is it about puppies?

Everybody has an opinion about puppies. Quickly. What's the first thing you think of when someone says "puppy?"

Most people will reply with "cute." A few of the more jaded readers will say, "work," or "barking" or even "pooper scooper."

But by and large people have a generally good feeling about puppies. Remember those old Pepsi commercials; the ones with the puppies jumping all over the little kids? They never once showed a soda in those commercials, just a laughing little boy and a pile of puppies. Flash the logo and fade to black and everyone has a good feeling about the soft drink.

Puppies are like magnets. People are just drawn to the little fur balls. And you can't help but smile and sometimes even laugh out loud as a clumsy little dog tries to get control of a bouncing tennis ball. Puppies are the inspiration for the cliché of the "warm and fuzzy" feeling. Don't ever put a puppy in the arms of a child and expect to go home without that dog. Once your kid gets hold of that puppy, you've bought it — even if you haven't paid for it yet.

But making a puppy part of your family takes some planning. Doing so also takes some commitment, and an investment of time. None of these events are overwhelming. They must, however, occur in the proper order. That is, you must first commit to getting a puppy. Only then can you plan effectively and prepare yourself to make the time investment the little dog will require.

Now, if I'm sounding like the overly conservative Dad, who always has to carry the bags of dog food, clean up the poop, hose out the kennels and take the dogs to the vet, that's because I am. But that doesn't make me the dream-crusher Dad, who says it can't be done, or it takes too much time or having a dog isn't worth the trouble. It can be done. It doesn't take too much time and it is worth every bit of trouble. But if you are going to do it, do it correctly. Commit. Plan. Invest. Then you can reap the rewards.

Commit

Committing to getting a puppy is not simply as easy as saying, "I'm getting a puppy." You have to start by assessing how and where you live. You have to really think about making time for the pet and handling all the details.

This is the part where those who have had a bad experience with a puppy in the past say that people considering a puppy should be *committed*. But after more than a decade of raising and training dogs, I wouldn't say it takes a mental health professional to handle a dog owner. Choosing to get a new puppy simply means that you first must look at your life — closely. Be

What is it about puppies? The list is too long to complete here.

honest. At first it will be a little bit of a chore — a chore with a happy ending, but a bit of chore nonetheless. You will have to do new things. You will change your schedule. Are you willing to make room, literally and figuratively, for a puppy? After you say yes, wait a week and ask yourself again. When you answer yes three times in a row you've got all the motivation you need to welcome a puppy into your life.

Plan

How can you take care of a dog? Do you keep an odd schedule? So what. Dogs are adaptable; the animal will learn to live its life around your day. Do you have lots of room for a dog to run or are you living in a one-room flat? Go to the library or log onto the Internet and study up on the breeds. You'll find out plenty of interesting facts that will only help you to improve your planning. Do you need a guard dog, a watchdog or a lap dog? What's the difference? Find out. Plan to get the kind of dog that seems like it will best fit with your lifestyle. Then buy the things the dog will need. Then, finally, buy the dog.

Invest

Puppies require time, but not as much time as you think. The best part is that the time you invest early on with the puppy will be paid back tenfold later on. Puppies are like little sponges. It only takes a matter of weeks to get them to do everything you want them to do. They are so simple to train that it almost seems too easy sometimes. If we get overconfident and expect too much from the pup, or get lax about training because the little guy is "doing so well," we might get frustrated. But that's not the dog's fault. I often tell people that training the trainer is the most important part of creating a great dog. I firmly believe that you can take the most wayward mutt of a puppy, provide love and care and praise and end up with the best, most loyal friend you've ever had. All you have to do is give the puppy a little bit of time each day and you will get complete devotion and obedience in return. Wouldn't it be great if everything worked that way?

So, why are you getting a puppy? Maybe it's none of my business, but it's a question you must answer before you go ahead and welcome the little bundle of energy into your home. There's one right reason to get a puppy: You really want a little furry friend. There are all kinds of other reasons — you want to teach your kids responsibility, you feel like you should have a watchdog, you want a hunting buddy or an exercise pal — but the whole issue boils down to the fact that you want a dog. Very few of us *need* dogs. We just

> Give the puppy a little bit of time each day and you will get complete devotion and obedience in return.

A good daily walk should provide all the exercise puppies need.

want dogs. You do want a dog, don't you? You see, now is the time to ask that question. Now is also the time to come up with an honest answer. So, give it some thought. I'll try to help you along here in the early parts of the book. First and foremost I can dispel the myth that dogs take up huge amounts of time. That's simply not true. You can have a well-trained dog by devoting just 15 minutes a day to your training. I would encourage you to spend as much time as you can with your puppy because this helps with the bonding process, but we all know that real life sometimes gets in the way. Even so, you can do it and have a great time with your new puppy even if you have some other things to do.

There is one very important consideration. Does everyone in the household want a puppy? If you have young children you know what their response will be. But what do the adolescents and your spouse think? It is funny how some people suddenly become allergic to dogs after they realize that there will some work involved. Owning dog is a family thing. Talk it over. Be realistic and remember that some people may not be as excited about this little fur ball as you are. A single person can own a puppy and care for it perfectly well, but that one person can have a much more difficult time if other members of their family are not so inspired by the pup. This is something important to think about.

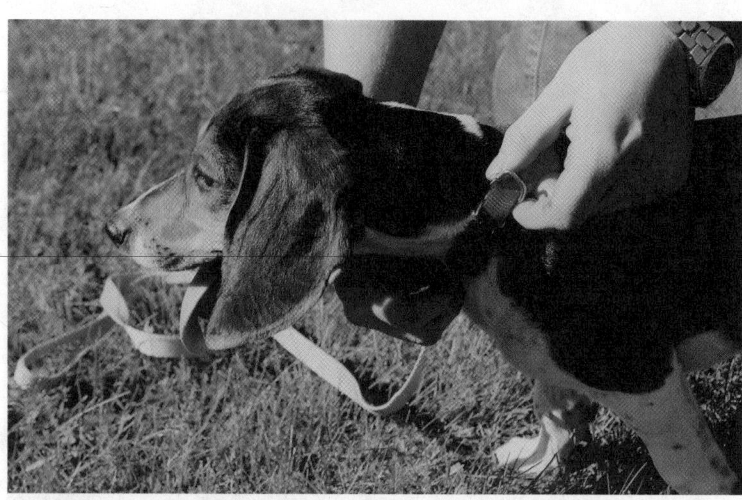

A good collar and a stout leash are the two basic ingredients for any training session. With them you have full control over the dog.

Here's the list

Puppies come with some requirements. You'll need things before you get a puppy. You'll want even more things after you get a puppy. That's all part of the fun. So, to get started, let's create a little checklist of things you absolutely must have before you get your puppy.

Mandatory Items

- Food (best to get the same kind your puppy is already eating)
- Food and water dishes
- Leash
- Collar
- Check cord
- Portable kennel (of the proper size)
- Pooper scooper
- Whistle

So there it is. With a little effort on your part you can use the items listed above and have a healthy, happy, well-mannered puppy. But that's boring, isn't it? Half the fun of getting a new puppy is buying the stuff you *need* for the furry little guy, right? So here's another list:

Secondary Items

- Chew toy
- Doggie treats
- Brush and comb
- Dog bed
- Doggie shampoo and conditioner
- Flea collar
- Fetch toys

The essentials are all here. Notice the Pet Porter is the right size.

A quality brush and shampoo are the basis of good dog grooming. Use them both often.

Buy a collar that fits. This one has reflective patches for walks in the morning and evening.

The details of the list are pretty important. You don't just need "stuff." You need the right stuff. Here's a closer look at the items on the list.

Collar: Measure the pup's neck and get a collar that fits. Collars are inexpensive, so buy the right size and replace worn collars right away. Nylon collars put up with all sorts of abuse. Leather collars are classy, but need care and "age" quickly. Of all the options for attaching the collar, the simple buckle works the best. If you walk after dark you can get a collar with reflective patches on it. There are more collars than there are dogs in this country. If it is durable and fits the puppy, it will work.

A good whistle is a great training aid. Get a couple—you will lose them.

Check cord: This is the long line used for controlling your puppy from a distance. You can buy one, but most are built for much bigger dogs. Make one that is light enough for puppies to pull around. You can make a suitable check cord by simply heading to the local hardware store and buying 20 feet of soft, yet stout, rope and a snap link.

Whistle: There are several good brands of dog whistles out there. Choose one you like and buy a couple of them because they will get lost. Get a couple good whistle lanyards and keep the whistle around your neck so it's always handy during training.

Dog box: Often called a portable kennel or a crate, this serves as a training device, a puppy bed and a safe means to transport the puppy in a vehicle. Again, get the right size. For your large breed pup, get a small box and move up to a bigger box as the dog grows.

Have the puppy chew on these instead of your best shoes, furniture, carpets, etc.

Buy a good quality dog bed and try hard to keep it clean.

Chew toys: Go with rawhide bones. The rawhide is good for the dog's teeth, inexpensive, and fairly durable.

Fetch toys: For puppies get the pint-sized dog training dummies. Never throw a stick for your dog. A dog, especially a puppy, running with a stick is an accident looking for a place to happen. Cuts to the mouth and potential injuries to the throat are severe and often require the attention of a veterinarian. Such an accident could cause the dog to avoid the game of fetch all together. What fun would that be?

Bedding: Get the high-end doggie pillows from one of the big catalog retailers. Better quality beds will last longer, will put up with more washings and will be more comfortable. *Consumer Reports* rates Drs. Foster and Smith dog beds the best in the country and they are made in America. And once you get that catalog you will be in dog stuff heaven. Keep control of those credit cards.

Training treats: I buy my training treats in bulk at the local wholesale club. There are all manner of treats on the market today. You can find anything from high-energy, all-meat snacks to meat-free, veggie snacks in case you and your companion have recently turned vegan. Buy the kind your dog likes and argue the merits of their nutrition later. But, no matter what kind you buy, use them wisely. And when I say "wisely" I mean for you to provide treats as an occasional training aid. Let the treat be a surprise or a reward for completion of particularly difficult task. If you give treats for every success, the puppy will soon learn to expect them and, like a spoiled child, will not perform without a bribe. Let praise be your biggest reward.

Dog food: Get the good stuff. While you can get away with bargain-basement treats, your dog's health depends on the nutrition you provide. While it would be easy

A quality dog dish should be right near the top of your list of things to buy for a new puppy. Steel never wears out and doesn't get chewed up.

to recommend one brand and finish this paragraph, food selection is more complicated. Ask your veterinarian about the type of food your dog needs. Many vets will recommend the stuff they sell, but you can dig deeper. Check out pet food websites. They offer lots of information, albeit about their brand. A great question is, "What type of food should my dog have?" Ask your vet to recommend the amount of protein your dog needs, how much fat is the right amount and what, if any, supplements you should provide.

Cleaning gear: There is no hiding the fact that puppies do what all dogs do. Puppies sometimes do it where they are not supposed to do it. It's your unsavory responsibility to clean up afterwards. Whether you choose a shovel, the ever-popular Pooper Scooper or the ubiquitous plastic bag, get used to the fact that feces occurs.

The collar and leash are the two finest training tools ever invented.

Toys, toys, toys: Later in the book, I'll tell you that the only "toy" you really need is something your puppy can safely fetch. After a quick count, I personally own 18 different "somethings" my dogs can safely fetch. One, in particular, comes to mind—The Flying Squirrel made by a company called Chuck It! It's a tough nylon rectangle with rubber corners that floats and flops in the air. I have never seen a dog, young or old, that didn't love to play with this thing. The only limit on puppy toys is durability. Puppies have needle-sharp teeth and the toys you buy had better stand up to those.

You'll notice I haven't included any canine medicines like wormer, shots and the like. I don't really lump them into the *items* you should buy. I consider them more like services rendered by your veterinarian. Later on we'll discuss the importance of maintaining a good schedule of veterinarian visits. For now, just know that you should also find a good vet.

As you can see, the list of items is not that long. Having a great puppy is more about what you do with the puppy than it is about what you buy for the animal. To keep things in perspective, people have been training and caring for dogs for hundreds of years without things like invisible fences and remote control electronic collars. These are great devices when used properly in a complete training program, but they are not requirements by any means.

All your puppy "stuff" should likely fit in a shopping bag. And that's good, because, at first, you are going to feel a bit overwhelmed, especially when the first few little things go wrong. Notice I said "when"—and not "if"—things go wrong. There will be some problems. With puppies, it will usually have to do with chewing and housebreaking. I will tell you how to handle both problems and the key will be self-control. When it comes to puppies, anger

What is the Best Age?

PHOTO BY JULIA JOHNSON

It is best to get a puppy early, ideally around 8 weeks of age. These guys will be ready to go soon.

One book claims that 49 days is the perfect—in fact, the only—age at which a new puppy should be taken home in order for the young dog to reach its full training potential. Well, let's get serious here. Very few of us will ever raise and train a field trial champion or a seeing-eye dog or a police dog. Our training regimen will be a bit less intense.

Most purebred puppies purchased from a breeder are taken home at between 8 and 10 weeks of age. This falls within the first part of what is known as the human socialization period, which lasts only until the dog is about 12 weeks old. This is the best time for a dog to learn to live with humans. At about the eighth week, puppies are forming permanent bonds. If allowed to remain with the litter, a puppy's primary bond will be with dogs rather than with people. This does not help training.

On the flip-side, if puppies are taken from their litter before they are 8 weeks old, proper canine socialization does not occur. If the puppy is taken away too early, it won't learn how to get along with other dogs. If this happens, the puppy can become a fighter or may bite out of fear and lash out at other dogs and people.

So, if you can't pick up your puppy during the eighth week, make sure humans are raising the pup until you can bring it home. Don't allow it to be left with the litter. You could end up with trouble in the long run.

is counter-productive. You'll see that statement often in this book. Anger is counter-productive. You won't teach your dog anything when you get angry. So, the goal will be to plan ahead to stop most of the problems before they start, and to simply go with the flow when you have a minor setback. Remember, this is supposed to be fun. You wanted a puppy, right? You had a good reason. Remember that reason when you are cleaning up after a pup that is just learning where to relieve itself.

The implications of your actions

It is one of the basic laws of the universe that for every action there is an equal and opposite reaction. This is especially true with very young puppies. Dogs freshly removed from their littermates are at their most impressionable. Everything is new and different. And everything is bigger than they are. Puppies can be traumatized very easily at this stage in their lives. They need, and deserve, care. You have made the choice to bring this young animal into your life and you've accepted all the responsibility that goes with it. Just what does that mean?

Here are a few things to think about. A puppy left alone undergoes a great deal of stress. For her entire life (all eight weeks) she has known nothing but the noise and interaction of a litter of fellow puppies. Now you and your family make up her entire pack. When you disappear, the puppy does not know if you'll return. There is no outlet for her energy. There is no one to provide simple direction and instruction as to what sights and sounds are safe and what should be avoided. If at all possible, take some time off work during the first week your new puppy is at home. Your training and care of the puppy will go much easier if your pup imprints on you without dealing with the stress and anxiety of daylong separations while you are at work.

If you can't take time away from work, at least try to make every effort to get home over lunch or have someone take care of the puppy during the day.

When it's training time, make sure the puppy knows that you are the boss. This situation could give the dog the wrong idea.

You will be required to do this during the housebreaking process anyway, and time spent with the pup early on will make training easier later.

At the same time you are working to spend more time with your puppy, you will also have to create a little bit of emotional distance or you will end up with a dog that has an acute case of separation anxiety. And, quite frankly, a dog that barks incessantly or chews everything in your house while you are gone is much more difficult to deal with than one that occasionally won't listen to a command.

The end result of good training is a dog that listens. This makes life much easier for everyone.

Let the puppy explore, but try to shield your puppy from torment by overly active kids or terrifying noises during the first few days at home. If you are hoping to have a hunting dog or a rough-and-tumble watchdog, make sure the puppy starts with plenty of outside time in all kinds of weather. Progressively rougher bouts of play (though still within the bounds of good manners) will help make the puppy bold. We'll discuss this more thoroughly in the training section, but for now rough play is good; hitting and yelling are bad.

Remember, the experiences your puppy has during the first few weeks will be imprinted on the dog for life. If you are a kind and caring dog owner who serves up fun and play along with gentle and directive discipline, your puppy will grow into a loyal, loveable, easily trained dog.

Naming rights

While the name you choose for your new puppy is not technically a care and training issue, the name can either assist with—or confuse—the commands you hope to use during training. Do you remember the comedian who named his dog Sit? Don't do that. Better yet, avoid most names beginning with S because it sounds like "sit." Go with a two-syllable name for your pup and make sure that it can't be confused with the basic commands: *Sit*, *Down*, *Come*, *Fetch*, *Heel* and *No*.

Names like Echo, Denver, Lucky and Oscar are appropriate because they work well with the aforementioned single-syllable commands. Say some of the combinations out loud and you'll notice how forceful the combination of a two-syllable name, followed by a one-syllable command, can be.

You realize, of course, the puppy doesn't really understand English. She's waiting to hear a sound (in this case a word) that will prompt her to act. The word might mean something to humans, but as far as the dog is concerned you could train it to respond to any word in the world, as long as you are consistent, and the dog will do so. That's right, if you want to say "hop" and have the dog sit when you say it, the training is pretty simple. So think about the name you are choosing for you dog, and not just in terms of how it fits the dog. Think also of how it will sound when you use it in conjunction with a command. If you name your dog Bo, you will first have to overcome the confusion of saying "Bo, no." Avoid that by going with two syllables.

The name game is also important if you have more than one dog. I always encourage people to say the name of the dog first, and then give the command. For example, "Echo, sit." Or "Buddy, come." Doing so teaches the dog to respond to her name and also gives her a chance to get ready for the upcoming command. When she hears her name, she knows a command is coming and she can focus on you. If you pause for just a couple seconds

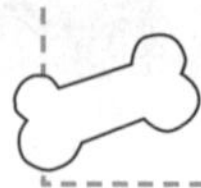

You realize, of course, the puppy doesn't really understand English.

between saying the name and giving the command you will see how the dog anticipates the command.

Owners with several dogs will find things much more relaxing if only one dog responds to each command. Think about it. If you have three dogs sitting in front of you when you throw a ball and you simply say, "fetch," you could end up with a melee on your hands. If, on the other hand, your early training has gone well you can say, "Lucky, fetch," and be reasonably sure only one dog is going to race after the ball.

Training takes consistency, repetition and a little bit of patience. Helping this training by making it as easy as possible for the puppy to understand you will make things a lit easier in the long run. "Speak" to the dog on its own terms, in a language it can understand, and you will be heard. The best part is, success is easy to see, especially with a puppy. You know you're doing it right when both you and the dog are happy during and after the training session.

Now that the technicalities are out of the way, there is the issue of image. You can let your five-year-old child name your Chesapeake Bay retriever "Fluffy," but does that really portray the image you want? There are actually several books with dog names out there. While the moniker you hang on

This is a big distraction to overcome. Good training will make it so these dogs listen when they really want to play.

> Your dog's name needs to reflect the way you and the dog will live, the things you'll do and the life you'll share together.

your puppy is not as important as the one given to a child, some thought should go into it. After all, this dog is supposed to be your pal, your partner, and your buddy. The name needs to reflect the way you and the dog will live, the things you'll do and the life you'll share together. In my humble opinion, a Doberman named Sissy just won't work. But now a poodle named Spike—that has a ring to it!

Puppy-proofing the home

Before bringing your puppy home, you'll need to "puppy-proof" any place to which the little guy will have access. Puppies are like babies: they want to explore every corner of your house, and they want to put everything into their mouths. They want to sniff and push and dig. It's not personal. Puppies are not trying to make you upset or get into dangerous situations. They are just acting out their genetics. They are just being dogs.

Here's a simple checklist to make sure your home is safe before letting the pup run free:

Secure the poisons — Make sure all poisonous household items are securely stored out of the puppy's reach. This includes household cleaners, laundry detergents, bleach, disinfectants, insecticides, cleaning fluid, fertilizers, mothballs, antifreeze, insect poisons, rat poisons and other items. Put them in high cabinets or on high shelves. These items can be deadly to your puppy.

Check your plants — Many plants in and around your house can be threatening to your pup. Did you know that the pits of apricots and peaches, as well as spinach and tomato vines, can make your puppy sick and, in large dosages, can even be fatal? See the sidebar on the next page for a list of common plants that can harm puppies. For a more complete list of plants that are dangerous to dogs, consult your vet.

Puppies chew. Better they chew on a toy than on something more expensive and more difficult to replace.

Problem Plants for Puppies

If your puppy has a tendency to nibble on grass, don't be alarmed. If his vegetarian habits continue and he tries to nibble on any of the following plants, STOP him, or you could have a few problems on your hands. These plants may make your puppy sick and may even kill him. Remember, this is not a complete list of dangerous plants. You'll need to talk with your vet to learn more about these and other plants that can be harmful to your pup.

Aloe Vera
Amaryllis
Apple (seeds)
Apple Leaf Croton
Apricot (pit)
Asparagus Fern
Autumn Crocus
Azalea

Baby's Breath
Bird of Paradise
Branching Ivy
Buckeye
Buddhist Pine

Caladium
Calla Lily
Castor Bean
Ceriman
Charming Dieffenbachia
Cherry (seeds and wilting leaves)
Chinese Evergreen
Cineraria
Clematis
Cordatum
Corn Plant
Cornstalk Plant
Croton
Cuban Laurel
Cutleaf Philodendron
Cycads
Cyclamen

Daffodil
Devil's Ivy
Dieffenbachia
Dracaena Palm
Dragon Tree
Dumb Cane

Easter Lily (esp. cats!)
Elaine
Elephant Ears
Emerald Feather
English Ivy
Eucalyptus

Fiddle-leaf Fig
Florida Beauty
Foxglove
Fruit Salad Plant

Geranium
German Ivy
Giant Dumb Cane
Glacier Ivy
Gold Dust Dracaena
Golden Pothos

Hahn's Self-Branching Ivy
Heartland Philodendron
Hurricane Plant

Indian Rubber Plant

Janet Craig Dracaena
Japanese Snow Lily (esp. cats!)
Jerusalem Cherry

Kalanchoe

Lacy Tree Philodendron
Lily of the Valley

Madagascar Dragon Tree
Marble Queen
Marijuana
Mexican Breadfruit
Miniature Croton
Mistletoe
Morning Glory
Mother-in-Law's Tongue

Narcissus
Needlepoint Ivy
Nephytis
Nightshade

Oleander
Onion
Oriental Lily (esp. cats!)

Peace Lily
Peach (wilting leaves and pits)
Pencil Cactus
Plumosa Fern
Poinsettia (low toxicity)
Poison Ivy
Poison Oak
Pothos
Precatory Bean
Primrose

Red Emerald
Red Princess
Red-Margined Dracaena
Rhododendron
Ribbon Plant

Saddle Leaf Philodendron
Sago Palm
Satin Pothos
Schefflera
Silver Pothos
Spotted Dumb Cane
String of Pearls
Striped Dracaena
Sweetheart Ivy
Swiss Cheese Plant

Taro Vine
Tiger Lily (esp. cats!)
Tomato Plant (green fruit, stem and leaves)
Tree Philodendron
Tropic Snow Dieffenbachia

Weeping Fig

Yew

Dog owners often overlook a simple first-aid kit. Get one.

Get a puppy's eye view — Get down on all fours and look around. It may seem silly at first, and you surely don't want the neighbors to catch you in such a position, but really look. Are there any dangling electric cords, loose nails, plastic bags or other tempting objects that will be in puppy's reach? If there are, cover them or put them away immediately.

Keep an eye on the pup — Never leave your puppy unsupervised inside or outside, and keep him off balconies, upper porches and high decks. Puppies are so little that they can easily slip through openings and fall. Puppies may also get tangled in ropes or the plastic from six-pack beverage holders. Keep these items away from puppies.

Keep your toilet lid down — Puppies are often tempted to play in toilet bowl water. This habit can be awful to break. Not only is it embarrassing when friends or family are visiting, but toilet cleanser may be harmful if swallowed.

Avoid electrocution — Unplug, remove or cover any electrical cords in your puppy's confinement area. Chewing on these cords can cause severe mouth burns, electrocution and fires. It is also a good idea to cover electrical outlets when they are not in use.

Do not tie ribbons around your puppy's neck — Not only does it look silly, the puppy may be tempted to chew the ribbon, which can cause digestive problems. He could also choke himself if he catches the ribbon on anything. Stick with a good, old-fashioned collar.

Watch the little things — Keep buttons, string, sewing needles, pins and other sharp objects out of your puppy's reach. If your puppy swallows any of these objects, he can damage his mouth and internal organs.

Kids and puppy care

First, it's great to share the responsibility of pet ownership with your children. However, it's important that you assign age-appropriate tasks. Here are a few examples of what you may expect:

Toddlers — A toddler can help parents with pet care simply by being involved – "helping" a parent fill food and water dishes, grooming, going with parents to take the pet for a walk, or to the veterinarian. Another good trick is to have the toddler give the dog a treat for good behavior. The toddler and the pet both enjoy this special job!

5 to 7 years old — This age group is capable of doing some of the tasks above (feeding, watering, grooming) without parental help. Still, you can't expect that a child this age will remember to do these jobs without friendly reminders from Mom or Dad. You might also need to supervise or check the progress of the work.

8 to 12 years old — Parents still need to supervise children in this age group for some tasks, like walking the dog. Before a child is 10 or 12 it's not advised that they walk a dog without adult supervision. But the child can feed, water and play with the pet alone (depending on the pet's temperament and the area available for exercising). Remember that kids this age sometimes get bored quickly. Make sure your child doesn't just "walk away" from the pet because something more fun has come up.

Teenagers — Depending on your teen's maturity, you can sometimes allow him/her to take full responsibility for the pet, including feeding them, cleaning up after them, driving them to the vet and exercising them. Allowing the teen to take the dog to obedience classes can also be a good activity for both the pet and the child. In many cases this is a great way to teach personal responsibility and to show that you believe in the abilities of the young person. You might still be called upon to handle some of the bills, but teenagers are often ready to move toward true pet ownership.

The list of what you'll *need* for a puppy is quite short. The things you'll *want* to buy could fill the back of a truck. Notice the two portable kennels. Puppies grow—get the right size at every age.

PHOTO BY JULIA JOHNSON

Chapter Two

Picking a Puppy

Let's face it, they're all cute. So, how do you go about getting the perfect puppy? If you are thinking of adding a roly-poly canine companion to your family, you must consider many factors in selecting the type of animal that best suits your lifestyle and fits your needs. The time and effort you invest in this important decision are just as important as the time and effort you will put into caring for and training your new friend. Remember, your pet will be a part of your life for up twelve years or more. You have some things to think about and some things to look for. You may have heard some of this before, but it's worth repeating.

If the parents are healthy, any of these pups will grow into a great dog.

Once you and your family have agreed you are ready to make a commitment to care for a puppy, you will need to decide what kind of dog is right for you. But, where do you begin your search? Your local animal shelter could be a good place to start. Animal shelters usually have a wide variety of puppies. Generally, these puppies receive careful medical exams and have already had initial vaccinations. Spaying or neutering is usually included in the adoption fee and can be performed when the animal reaches the appropriate age. Most shelters have excellent support services such as free behavioral counseling. And, if you factor in the reality of what will happen to these dogs if they don't find a home…well, making such a choice might be easier.

You may also wish to talk to local dog trainers, or groomers. You can also contact reputable breeders and obtain advice from a practicing veterinarian in your search for that perfect puppy.

Just remember to consider your lifestyle. Breeds such as hunting or working dogs require more exercise than some smaller breeds and may crowd an apartment or small home. Do you have a fence to contain your new companion? What about grooming? Keep in mind that almost all dogs shed their hair coat at least twice per year (spring and fall). Some kinds of dogs shed constantly and some breeds have to be professionally groomed. Groomers can provide further information on which breeds possess which traits. There are also other considerations.

Any puppy or dog can make a great pet if the owners take the time to properly socialize and train it.

Purebred vs. mixed breed

I've seen lots of dogs and a wide variety of dog owners. One of the most commonly asked questions is "Which dog makes a better pet, the mixed breed or the purebred?" The truth is any puppy or dog can make a great pet if the owners take the time to properly socialize and train it. I've seen a pit bull/Labrador mix that was one of the finest pheasant hunting dogs around, and I've watched dogs from "champion stock" destroy home interiors just because they hated to be alone.

Let's start with the most popular dog in America—the mixed breed. They come in all shapes and sizes, they can be short- or long-coated, they are available in many colors and they can make wonderful companions. As suggested earlier, your local shelter is an excellent source for obtaining a mixed-breed puppy. If you are simply looking for a loving companion, look no

Mixed-breed puppies can make great pets and will respond to good training the same as a show champion…sometimes even better.

further than your local shelter to begin enjoying the life-enriching benefits of pet ownership.

I recently read a story about stray dogs in Egypt that said with unregulated breeding, mixed-breed dogs will all—after a few generations—end up as short-haired, multi-colored animals with an upturned, bushy tail and rather pointy facial features. These dogs will all weigh about 30 to 35 pounds when full grown and will tend to be active and energetic. Apparently, these animals are very much like the first dogs domesticated by humans thousands of years ago.

Most mixed-breed dogs you encounter in this country are not far removed from purebreds and tend to retain some of the traits of their ancestral breeds. Thus, it is valuable to find out what kind of genes the dog you like is carrying. If the puppy is mostly Siberian husky, you'll have an animal that likes to run and needs some room to roam. Hounds bark—that is their job. Do some research and try to figure out what you're getting into.

One of the benefits of getting a mixed-breed dog is that genetic problems inherent with some types of purebreds may not show up with a mixed breed, while some of the breed's desirable traits are retained. On the other hand, there are very likely no controls on breeding programs, so you really don't know what you'll end up with. If you decide to adopt a puppy from the shelter, get the youngest one you can and get one that has spent the shortest amount of time in the shelter. Dogs that have spent a long time in a shelter can be somewhat hyperactive, and can be distant and difficult to train. This all comes back to proper socialization, or lack thereof.

> Deciding what kind of dog to get is as important as deciding whether to get a dog in the first place.

The purebred puppy

Deciding what kind of dog to get is as important as deciding whether to get a dog in the first place, and your choices of purebred puppies can be somewhat overwhelming. The American Kennel Club recognizes more than 150 different breeds of dog (see the Appendix on page 162), and each breed has its own unique temperament, appearance, activity level and set of needs. Our handy review of popular breeds is great place to start learning more about the various breeds and their attributes, but get ready to do some serious research to determine exactly which puppy might be the best fit for your family's lifestyle. The Internet is a great resource for aspiring dog owners, and your local library, your favorite bookstore or the book departments of pet specialty stores should all have books profiling various breeds of dogs. The Bibliography and Resources section on page 165 suggests a few titles.

As you do your research, remember that hounds bark, sled dogs run and some breeds were bred to be more aggressive than others. Every dog

Do your research and get a dog that fits your lifestyle. This small puppy will someday be a much bigger adult needing lots of exercise.

has a job and you can't expect to "train away" centuries of breeding and instinct. For example, if you regularly have a large group of small children at your home, you may not want to get a herding dog. I've seen shelties and Australian shepherds circle around the perimeter of a group of little kids nipping at heels and generally trying to keep all the young ones together. While it sounds good in theory, you can get some pretty frustrated, and perhaps scared, little kids as a result.

Here are some things to consider as you research purebred puppies:

Temperament

You're going to be living with this dog for a long time, so you need to make sure he has a personality you can live with. Do you want a dog that is active, or subdued? A dog that is easily trained, or strong-willed? A dog that is friendly to everyone he meets, or one that is loyal to family but aloof toward strangers? Do you desire a dog that needs a lot of attention from family members, and lots of activity to prevent him from becoming bored and destructive, or a dog that is content to be left alone for periods of time

PHOTO BY JULIA JOHNSON

This little guy looks small right now, but someday he's going to be a lot bigger. Don't forget to plan for his full-grown size when you think about taking him home.

during the day? This last concern can—to some extent—be addressed with training and proper mental conditioning, but it could be an issue.

Size

All puppies are adorable, but they grow quickly—and some of them grow a lot. Find out how large—in height and weight—that cute puppy will become before you bring him home. Larger dogs require more food and space—is your yard or living room big enough to meet his needs? Keep in mind that some little dogs still need lots of room to run around and burn off energy.

Coat/Grooming Needs

All dogs need to be groomed regularly to stay healthy and clean, and most dogs will shed. Some dogs will shed only a little bit, and some shed in clumps for just a few weeks, but some dogs shed profusely all year round. Long-coated dogs are beautiful to look at, but require a lot of effort to stay that way. Short-coated dogs are easier to care for, but may still shed, and may require protection in cold or wet weather. Dogs with fancy trims may need professional grooming. Decide how much dog hair you're willing to put up with, and how much time and energy you can afford to invest in coat care, when you're deciding which breed is right for you.

Male or Female

In general, there is no significant difference in temperament between male and female dogs. If you are getting a dog for a pet, you will want to have your dog spayed or neutered, which will eliminate most minor differences anyway. If you plan to show or breed your dog, you must be vigilant about preventing unwanted breedings by keeping your intact male safely confined to your house or yard, and by keeping your intact female away from other dogs when she comes into heat twice yearly.

Health

Some breeds may be prone to hereditary diseases or conditions. Many breeds can be screened for certain conditions, such as hip or eye problems; this certification should be available to you when you go to look at a puppy. Being educated about the health considerations of your chosen breed can help you to avoid or alleviate future problems.

The time has come

If you are going to pick your purebred puppy from the litter, you may be agonizing over how you should make the choice. Do you want the biggest, boldest puppy in the group, or do you want the runt? Is there one puppy that barks or whines a lot? Where's the quiet one?

Who could turn down this face? If you've done your homework and found he has great parents, you can take him home with confidence.

PHOTO BY JULIA JOHNSON

If this mother has all the traits you want in a dog, there's a good chance her puppies will make great pets, too. Remember, choose the right parents to get the puppy you want.

Well, if you follow these directions, choosing a puppy from a litter should be the easiest part of the process. You see, with a purebred dog, you don't really choose the puppy, you choose the parents. That's right. What you want from your purebred puppy are the attributes that come from the parents. You should ask to see them both and they must both fit the breed standard (that's available from the AKC) and they should be in good health. Look for things like clear eyes, good muscle tone, healthy activity levels and a smooth, even gait. There is also the issue of attitude. Dogs should be friendly. Even well-trained guard dogs are friendly until given the proper commands. The parents should like people, and be confident among them. If you are hoping to create a hunting companion from your puppy, the parents should be from hunting stock and it's better if they also hunt. Don't try to put a show ring champion in the field. It won't work.

You also want to make sure the breeder has a fairly clean and well-kept kennel. If the kennels are clean and well maintained, you can likely bet the dogs are not lacking in care, either.

Now, after all this research, you are ready to go get your puppy. If the parents are good, well-mannered dogs and meet with your approval, just select the sex you want, close your eyes and grab a puppy. They are all cute anyway. And the rest is really up to you. All the socialization and training

With a purebred dog, you don't really choose the puppy, you choose the parents.

> There are really not that many major differences in raising and training a male or a female dog.

will be up to you. If you pick the runt, you can feed him up to get him as big as the breed can get. If the pup you get is a little bit timid, your training can make him bold.

Closing your eyes and grabbing a puppy might be an over-simplification, but not by much. If you really feel like you should have one particular puppy from a litter, try running a few little tests. Roll a ball near the litter and see which one goes for it. Grab a puppy and roll her over. A puppy that struggles will be bit more stubborn than one that's simply submissive. Whistle and see which one responds. Bend over, clap your hands and see which dog pulls away from the group. There are a million little tests and if they mean something to you, then by all means utilize them. But remember to check over the parents. That's where good puppies start.

As far as the sex of your dog — there really are not that many major difference in raising and training a male or female dog. It is worth repeating that if you don't plan to include the dog in an organized and well-planned breeding program, you should have the animal spayed or neutered and you'll have one less thing to worry about. When it comes to training don't think that male dogs are more stubborn and don't believe that female dogs have less desire to hunt or work. All dogs, regardless of their sex, will perform to the level of their training and respond to the style of their trainer. Like I said a few paragraphs up, it's all up to you.

Which breed is right for you?

In this age of overwhelming amounts of information, you can find out just about anything you want to know with just the click of a button. There are dozens of web sites, hundreds of books and millions of people with opinions about which dog is the best and what it will be like to own and care for a certain breed. Honestly, there are no pat answers. The dog responds to its trainer and its surroundings. A Chesapeake Bay Retreiver living on a farm in North Dakota will not be exactly like the Chessie living in suburban Detroit or the one living at a duck hunting camp in eastern Washington State.

But, there are certain attributes for each breed that potential owners should know about. For this section I've assembled a sampling of popular breeds and briefly outlined some general information from things I've picked up over the years and from people who talk about their dogs. This is by no means the last word on these dogs. Nor should it be considered the only word. These notes are just a starting point. Much more research is required before you make the 10-year commitment to owning a dog. Start here, but read more and learn more.

A Review of Popular Breeds

Akita

Temperament: While affectionate with its family, the Akita is very aggressive to other dogs. Intelligent, and fearless, it is a first-class guard dog, but needs firm training as a puppy. Extremely faithful and enjoys companionship.

Health Issues: Prone to immune diseases like VKH and to hip dysplasia.

Life Span: 10-12 years.

Housing and Exercise: Will do well in an apartment if it is exercised often. It is active indoors and will do best with a large yard.

Alaskan Malamute

Temperament: Friendly, good-natured breed that is usually good with children and strangers. Strong-willed and confident; tends to be very stubborn and early obedience training is a must.

Health Issues: Susceptible to hip dysplasia, and eye problems.

Life Span: 10-12 years.

Housing and Exercise: Needs lots of space. A house with a large fenced yard with some shade is essential.

American Bulldog

Temperament: Outstandingly obedient and truly loyal to its master if trained properly. Eager to please, and genuinely loves children. Known to be assertive and bold. Happiest when it has a job to do.

Health Issues: Prone to hip dysplasia.

Life Span: Up to 16 years.

Housing and Exercise: Inactive indoors and requires a yard and moderate exercise outside.

American Pit Bull Terrier

Temperament: With proper training, can be loyal and well mannered. But has been known to be aggressive, especially to other dogs. When properly socialized, makes good family pet and intimidating guard dog.

Health Issues: Usually healthy, but some may be allergic to grass.

Life Span: About 12 years.

Housing and Exercise: A good fence is called for. Has lots of energy and needs supervision. Only as good as its owner.

Australian Shepherd

Temperament: Intelligent, clever and devoted. Eager to please and easy to train. Affectionate and active; makes an excellent children's companion.
Health Issues: Susceptible to hip dysplasia, blindness and deafness.
Life Span: 12-15 years.
Housing and Exercise: Needs frequent exercise and always does best with room to roam. Happiest when it has a job to do, whether it's herding sheep or keeping an eye on kids. Great breed for agility or obedience training and competition.

Basset Hound

Temperament: Fits well into family life and is well-behaved, but it may be stubborn. With proper training, they are obedient, but when they pick up scent, they may not listen to commands.
Health Issues: Do not overfeed because extra weight places a load on the legs and spine that can leave the dog lame. Prone to bloat.
Life Span: 10-12 years.
Housing and Exercise: Will do okay in an apartment, but very inactive indoors. Outdoors, expect hours of play. Exercise is needed to keep them healthy and trim, but in moderation—with their short legs, walking is much better than running.

Beagle

Temperament: Has a cheerful, upbeat personality and is great with kids. Like all scent hounds, is independent and will always "follow their noses"—ignoring your protests to return. Teach the dog to come early.
Health Issues: Susceptible to epilepsy, glaucoma, and heart disease.
Life Span: Expected life span is 12-15 years.
Housing and Exercise: Needs companionship and daily exercise. Bred to hunt and drive game and may be difficult to break of that. Prone to barking and howling; do not make good apartment dogs.

Bernese Mountain Dog

Temperament: Gets along well with, and is extremely loyal to, its family and often attaches itself to one member. Eager to please and easy to train. Intelligent and loving and makes an excellent family dog. May be slow to mature and have puppy-like habits well after other dogs have "grown up."

Health Issues: Can suffer from hip dysplasia, hereditary eye diseases, intestinal disorders and cancer.

Life Span: About 6-8 years.

Housing and Exercise: Not a dog for apartments. Requires a large yard in a cooler climate.

Bichon Frise

Temperament: Very perky and playful. Gets along well with strangers, small children and other dogs and pets, but will often bark a lot.

Health Issues: Susceptible to skin and ear problems, epilepsy and leg problems.

Life Span: Will often live 12-15 years.

Housing and Exercise: Does well in apartments, but should be walked about twice a day.

Boxer

Temperament: Energetic, attentive and devoted dog that is gentle with children. Behaves well with other household pets, but cautious with strange pets and people. Can make good guard dog.

Health Issues: Susceptible to hip dysplasia, cancer (in older dogs), allergies and heart problems .

Life Span: 8-10 years.

Housing and Exercise: Full of energy; perfect companion for active families. Requires mental and physical exertion and not recommended for people who are easy going and slow moving. Sensitive to hot and cold weather. Does best when allowed to divide time between the house and the yard.

Brittany

Temperament: Highly energetic and friendly. Good-natured. Does well with children and other pets. Can be soft; harsh training is not recommended.

Health Issues: Susceptible to hip dysplasia and seizures.

Life Span: 12-13 years.

Housing and Exercise: Very energetic; enjoys a big yard. Gets nervous if not given enough exercise. An excellent breed for the hunter who also wants a family pet.

Bulldog

Temperament: Friendly and good-natured—an almost mellow dog that is very good with children. May be aggressive with strange dogs, but usually gets along well with other pets.

Health Issues: Susceptible to breathing and whelping difficulties, and overheating .
Life Span: Most live 8-10 years.
Housing and Exercise: Needs little exercise to remain happy. Good apartment dogs; a walk each day will provide enough exercise. Should not be made to run or walk long distances in hot weather.

Cavalier King Charles Spaniel

Temperament: Gentle dogs that will cower if treated heavily. Respond much better to positive training. A lap dog that, given a choice, would always choose the company of groups of people.
Health Issues: Susceptible to breathing problems, heart disease (MVD), eye problems and ear infections.
Life Span: 10-12 years.
Housing and Exercise: Needs very little exercise. Should also be kept away from very hot or extremely cold conditions.

Chesapeake Bay Retriever

Temperament: Protective breed that will serve as a solid watchdog—yet is loyal to family and easy to train. Makes a good family pet if raised from a pup in a loving home with firm rules.
Health Issues: Susceptible to eye diseases and hip dysplasia.
Life Span: 10-13 years.
Housing and Exercise: Inactive indoors. Bred to hunt the icy waters of Chesapeake Bay; deserves to be challenged physically. Should sleep outdoors because that's what it likes.

Chihuahua

Temperament: Makes a wonderful companion, but is sometimes timid around new people—because of this, makes a good watchdog.
Health Issues: Susceptible to leg and eye problems.
Life Span: Can live 15 or more years.
Housing and Exercise: Takes well to apartment life, but can be noisy. Needs little exercise, but very playful.

Chow Chow

Temperament: Smart and protective. Most will be loyal to only a few people, and likely to be very aggressive toward other dogs. The owner should be an experienced dog handler and be prepared to handle this sometimes stubborn and aggressive breed.
Health Issues: Like most bigger dogs, can suffer hip dysplasia.
Life Span: 8-12 years.
Housing and Exercise: Needs lots of exercise and should be fenced to help keep them from other dogs.

Cocker Spaniel

Temperament: Lovable little dogs. Perfect for the whole family, but can become jealous when new children are brought into the home.

Health Issues: Sometimes suffer from ear infections, hip dysplasia and epilepsy. Find a reputable breeder and watch for eye trouble.

Life Span: Most live 12-15 years.

Housing and Exercise: Adapts well to any environment, but needs plenty of exercise. Loves to chase tennis balls.

Collie

Temperament: Highly intelligent, sensitive, loyal and easy to train. Usually tolerates other dogs. Very devoted.

Health Issues: Generally healthy, but some are prone to PRA, eye defects and hip problems leading to arthritis.

Life Span: 14-16 years.

Housing and Exercise: Will do well in an apartment with plenty of exercise. Provide shade and fresh water in warm weather. Inactive indoors; needs a yard.

Dachshund

Temperament: Defined by their coats: smooth-haired are typically friendly; longhaired can be leery of strangers; and wirehaired can be stubborn.

Health Issues: Susceptible to eye diseases and skin problems.

Life Span: 12-14 years.

Housing and Exercise: Can sometimes be noisy, but will live in apartments as long as they get lots of exercise and attention.

Dalmatian

Temperament: Loves its owner, but can be tough to train because it gets so excited at times.

Health Issues: Many are deaf thanks to indiscriminate breeding. Can also suffer urinary tract problems and skin ailments.

Life Span: 12-14 years.

Housing and Exercise: Loves to run and play. Get ready to put on your walking shoes—these dogs need to get out and move around.

Doberman Pinscher

Temperament: Intense, intelligent and energetic, yet easy to train. Assertive, but not vicious. Still, all family members should be able to handle the dog. Should be thoroughly socialized.

Health Issues: Generally healthy, but prone to bloat, hip dysplasia, congenital heart disorders and obesity in middle age.

Life Span: 11-13 years.

Housing and Exercise: Very cold sensitive; not an outside dog. Will do well in an apartment if exercised.

English Springer Spaniel

Temperament: Another true family dog. A quick learner that loves people.

Health Issues: Can suffer epilepsy, ear infections and eye problems.

Life Span: 10-14 years.

Housing and Exercise: Should have daily exercise. As a dog developed for hunting upland game, has boundless energy that should be put to good use.

Fox Terrier

Temperament: Can be playful and loving, or feisty and quick to bite. Supervise this dog around children and other pets. Make excellent watchdogs because they bark a lot.

Health Issues: Prone to epilepsy and shoulder problems. Very light-colored dogs show higher rates of deafness.

Life Span: Will live 15 or more years.

Housing and Exercise: Bred to hunt and will chase smaller animals—walk on a leash every day.

German Shepherd Dog

Temperament: Highly intelligent, territorial, devoted and faithful. Initially suspicious of strangers. A great watchdog that can be trained to handle just about any job.

Life Span: 10-12 years.

Health Issues: Susceptible to skin disease, bloat, heart problems and hip dysplasia. Enormous popularity has led to careless breeding, resulting in a number of crippling genetic problems within the breed. Look for a reputable breeder.

Housing and Exercise: Needs exercise and daily mental challenges. Makes good housedog, although a fenced yard and plenty of stimulation is required.

German Shorthaired Pointer

Temperament: A ball of energy and intelligence. Makes a good family dog, but sometimes rough with small children and smaller pets. Like most pointers, likes to roam and search.

Health Issues: Bigger dogs are susceptible to hip dysplasia. Can also suffer epilepsy. Because of the popularity of the dog, look for a good breeder.

Life Span: 12-14 years.

Housing and Exercise: Needs to hunt. Can live in the city, but offer lots of exercise and games.

Giant Schnauzer

Temperament: Great with kids when taught by an experienced trainer. Stubborn.

Health Issues: Usually very healthy.

Life Span: 12-15 years.

Housing and Exercise: Needs to play every day. Really enjoys roughhousing and running around.

Golden Retriever

Temperament: Loving and gentle. Will not take well to heavy-handed training. Great with children and can be trained to be wonderful assistance dogs.

Health Issues: Can suffer skin and thyroid problems, eye trouble and hip dysplasia.

Life Span: 10-13 years.

Housing and Exercise: Hunting dog, bred to flush and retrieve game birds. Needs challenges and active human companionship, not confinement in apartments.

Great Dane

Temperament: Despite its size, is very active and plays well with children if watched closely. Tough to train; be firm.

Health Issues: Can suffer intestinal troubles, hip dysplasia, and heart problems.

Life Span: 6-8 years.

Housing and Exercise: Relatively inactive inside, but often quite active outdoors. Give this giant lots of room.

Great Pyrenees

Temperament: Loyal, and a good watchdog, but difficult to train. Firmness and patience are the orders of the day.

Health Issues: Can suffer hip dysplasia and epilepsy.

Life Span: 10-12 years.

Housing and Exercise: Should have a country home, ideally with something to watch over. Needs daily exercise.

Greyhound

Temperament: Makes great companion, but can be timid. Often becomes devoted to their families. Dogs off the track are easy to housebreak and make great pets.

Health Issues: Can get sores lying on hard surfaces. Should be fed two or three small meals each day.

Life Span: 10-12 years.

Housing and Exercise: Should be allowed to run around daily. Can do well in an apartment as long as they have solid routine and exercise.

Irish Setter

Temperament: Wonderful family dog, friendly and smart. But because of their popularity, bad breeding has made some of them high-strung. Must be trained young.

Health Issues: Susceptible to bloat, epilepsy and eye problems

Life Span: 11-15 years.

Housing and Exercise: Roaming dog originally bred to range widely to find game. Loves to run and should be allowed to do so often. Make sure you teach this dog its basic commands well.

Irish Terrier

Temperament: Loves children, and will protect them with great vigor. But, doesn't like other dogs around and will fight with them given the chance. Keep on a leash to keep under control.

Health Issues: Almost always healthy.

Life Span: 12-15 years.

Housing and Exercise: Can live in an apartment, but does better with more space. Requires firm training and control, especially out in public.

Jack Russell Terrier

Temperament: Confident, but also seems to enjoy training. This attitude serves well in the field as a hunter or in the home as a playmate.

Health Issues: Typically healthy, but some dogs suffer eye problems and bad knees.

Life Span: 13-15 years.

Housing and Exercise: Enjoys space for play, but can live in an apartment if walked daily.

Labrador Retriever

Temperament: A true all-around dog. Easy to train, great with children and willing to do just about anything. Has found work in hunting fields, on police forces, and on back porches around the world.

Health Issues: If not the product of good breeding, is susceptible to hip dysplasia, epilepsy and eye diseases.

Life Span: 10-12 years.

Housing and Exercise: Needs to work to be happy and healthy. Loves to find things and fetch them, especially in the water. A very capable and versatile hunting companion, or a great partner for just about any kind of outdoor activity.

Lhasa Apso

Temperament: Very friendly and smart, but dislikes strangers and makes an excellent watchdog.

Health Issues: Sometimes suffers from hip dysplasia and skin, kidney and eye problems.

Life Span: 12-14 years.

Housing and Exercise: Can be very active indoors. A walk each day will provide plenty of exercise.

Mastiff

Temperament: Bred as a watchdog that will be happy and friendly with family members.

Health Issues: Because of its large size, is susceptible to bone and heart problems. Some dogs suffer from bloat, depending on their diet.

Life Span: 8-10 years.

Housing and Exercise: Does best in a house with a fenced yard. The owner should be a strong and confident leader to keep the Mastiff from becoming spoiled and pushy.

Newfoundland

Temperament: A family dog through and through. Is suspicious of strangers, but kind and caring around family members.

Health Issues: Susceptible to hip dysplasia and hereditary heart problems.

Life Span: 8-10 years.

Housing and Exercise: Needs space and does not like too much heat. Yet, these gentle giants are very active; avoid if you live in a warm climate.

Nova Scotia Duck Tolling Retriever

Temperament: Playful, happy and easy to train. Typically barks very little and seems to really love being near children.

Health Issues: Susceptible to eye trouble and thyroid problems.

Life Span: 12-14 years.

Housing and Exercise: Having been bred on the coasts of Canada, enjoys cool weather and loves the chance to swim. Needs plenty of exercise and will fetch for as long as you are willing to throw an object.

Old English Sheepdog

Temperament: Was once actually used to herd sheep; now most often kept simply as pets. Loves to play with children and will often circle groups of kids in an effort to "herd" them.

Health Issues: Prone to hip dysplasia and cataracts.

Life Span: 10-12 years.

Housing and Exercise: Loves to play and run, and requires plenty of room. Sheds and requires plenty of grooming.

Pomeranian

Temperament: Makes a good companion and enjoys being a lap dog, but tend to bark—a lot—at strangers and other animals.

Health Issues: Susceptible to tooth problems.

Life Span: 12-16 years.

Housing and Exercise: Suitable for all environments, whether it be in a house, apartment, city or country. Enjoys an active family atmosphere. Can be a great companion for the elderly.

Poodle (Toy)

Temperament: Good-tempered and devoted to its family. While affectionate with their owners, can be timid with new people.
Health Issues: Susceptible to leg problems, epilepsy, ear infections, eye disease and diabetes.
Life Span: 12-14 years.
Housing and Exercise: Does well in apartments and good dog for less-active people. One walk a day is fine. Poodles come in three sizes. From largest to smallest they are: standard, miniature and toy. Standard poodles were originally retrieving dogs, but all members of the breed are now considered show dogs. There are very few working poodles left.

Portuguese Water Dog

Temperament: Intelligent. Originally bred to guard Portuguese fishing boats, carry messages and retrieve anything that fell overboard. Gets along well with children and other dogs, and is quite loyal. Responds well to tone of voice.
Health Issues: Susceptible to hip dysplasia. Breeding stock should be tested for GM-1 Storage Disease, a fatal nerve disease that appears when a puppy is 6 months old.
Life Span: 10-14 years.
Housing and Exercise: Does well in an apartment as long as it gets lots of exercise. In temperate climates can live outside, but likes to be close to people. Loves to retrieve and does not shed. Has curly hair and should be groomed often.

Rhodesian Ridgeback

Temperament: Originally bred for fighting lions. Can withstand the harsh desert heat and is not bothered by bugs. Loyal and obedient. Makes a good guard dog.
Health Issues: Susceptible to hip dysplasia, dermoid sinus, and cysts.
Life Span: 10-12 years.

Housing and Exercise: Can live in an apartment, but requires tons of exercise. Seems to never get tired. Perfect if you need a watchdog and love to exercise.

Rottweiler

Temperament: Very territorial and imposing, ideal for protection. Requires strong leadership and firm training.

Health Issues: Susceptible to hip dysplasia, bloat and parvo virus. Popularity has led to careless breeding, resulting in a number of problems within the breed.

Life Span: 8-11 years.

Housing and Exercise: Needs plenty of exercise and activity. Because it dislikes newcomers, should not be kept where people often pass by.

Saint Bernard

Temperament: Very gentle and friendly, but must be obedience trained early because it gets so big. Should get daily exercise and have plenty of room to roam.

Health Issues: Susceptible to heart problems, skin problems and hip dysplasia.

Life Span: 8-10 years.

Housing and Exercise: Does best with lots of room and time spent outside. Tends to be lethargic indoors. Even so, prefers to be near people.

Scottish Terrier

Temperament: A confident little dog that that can serve as a watchdog. May be cool toward strangers and aggressive with other dogs.

Health Issues: May suffer from flea allergy and skin problems.

Life Span: 11-13 years.

Housing and Exercise: Does well in an apartment as long as it gets plenty of exercise.

Shetland Sheepdog

Temperament: Loyal, affectionate and very responsive to training. Can be shy around strangers. Alert and protective, making it a good watchdog.

Health Issues: Susceptible to Dermatomyositis (Sheltie Skin Syndrome), thyroid disease and hip dysplasia.

Life Span: 12-14 years.

Housing and Exercise: Needs daily walks and active play time, but will adapt to just about any lifestyle. Loves obedience training and competition.

Weimaraner

Temperament: Affectionate and very rambunctious. Intelligent, but can be willful, and should have firm training from the start. Socialize them well at an early age.

Health Issues: May suffer hip dysplasia, but are generally a hardy breed of dog. Prone to bloat, so feed several small meals, not one big one.

Life Span: 10- 13 years.

Housing and Exercise: Needs plenty of opportunities to run free and lots of regular exercise. Relatively inactive indoors; will do best with a large yard. Do not exercise after meals.

Welsh Corgi (Cardigan)

Temperament: A fun-loving dog that very much wants to be part of a family. Intelligent, obedient and protective; does not immediately trust strangers.

Health Issues: Susceptible to back disorders, glaucoma and epilepsy.

Life Span: 12-15 years.

Housing and Exercise: Adaptable to a number of environments. Does well in apartments, but should be given plenty of exercise. Loves walks and playtime—fetch with a ball is a particular favorite.

Yorkshire Terrier

Temperament: Thinks it is bigger than it really is, but only up to a point. Usually timid around strangers and doesn't like rough play. Tends to bark a lot more than it should.

Health Issues: Susceptible to eye irritations, tracheal collapse, tooth problems and leg trouble.

Life Span: 14-16 years.

Housing and Exercise: Less active than other terriers, and doesn't need much exercise. But, even one long walk a day won't quiet it down if it's excited.

Chapter Three

The First Days at Home

When the day finally arrives that you get to take your new pup home, you can expect to be only slightly less worried than a new parent. But don't panic. Bringing home a new puppy is nothing like bringing home a new baby. By now you should have all your new puppy stuff in place and ready to go. Remember that shopping list back in Chapter 1? All those bases should be covered. Anything you buy above and beyond that is just for the pure joy and excitement that comes with getting the stuff you "need" when you get a new dog. Like buying toys for a new baby, the cool stuff you buy for a new puppy will never be wasted. Someday you'll use it—or give it to a friend who'll use it. If getting the stuff makes you happy, go get it. That's what having a dog is all about.

Your puppy's big adventure is about to start. Make sure you are ready to give her the safe, happy home she needs.

And it starts...

Dog ownership really begins as you take your new puppy to the car for the drive home. Give the little guy a sense of security by carrying him to the car, especially if the puppy is just 8 weeks old and leaving his littermates for the first time. Support the puppy's belly and wrap your arm around him to let him know that everything will be just fine.

All dogs should ride in portable kennels for every trip in the car or truck. Having said that, I acknowledge that some of you will break that rule eventually. But at least start with a good portable kennel of the proper size for your pup. Read that again. See that last part? The proper size for your pup means just that. Get the small portable kennel first, and then move up as the dog grows. With some breeds you may have to buy two or three different kennels during the first year. Once the dog is full grown, you can stop investing in kennels. Until then, the proper size will help to keep your dog safe and provide a feeling of security in the moving vehicle.

There are lots of good reasons to keep a puppy in a portable kennel during a ride in the car. The first is control. If the puppy is secured inside the kennel, you know where the animal is at all times. Therefore, you don't have to take your eyes off the road to see if the little guy is chewing your fine leather seats or pushing his way onto your lap for a better view of the steering column. There is also the issue of cleanliness. I'm not that worried about the puppy shedding all over the upholstery, but some young dogs get carsick. That's not something you want deposited in your lap as you try to merge into the fast lane. While a puppy is inside a kennel of the proper size, he will consider the container his den and not urinate or defecate in there. That's another big bonus. Finally, you are providing some very early and basic separation training. The dog can hear you and see you, but doesn't have to be right on your lap. So, he will come to understand that being away from you (at this point you represent the puppy's only friend in a big new world) is nothing to be afraid of.

Place a pad and a small soft blanket inside the kennel for the first drive home. If everything goes as planned, your pup should fall asleep during the drive and you'll soon have an animal that is calm and content riding in a vehicle.

If everything doesn't go as planned, consider it a training session. If your pup gets upset during the drive, you have to ignore it. An agitated puppy is seeking attention, but your attention will be the reward for unwanted behavior. If you reward the behavior of a dog—any behavior—you will see it repeated. So, if your puppy gets upset during a ride in the car, talk softly to her. Try to reassure her that everything is going well and you are still around. If the whining and barking don't stop, you'll just have to endure the noise until they do. The one thing you must not do is take her out of the kennel. I'll repeat that. Do not take the dog out of the kennel because she is whining or crying or barking or panting. Again, if you reward the behavior, it will be repeated. With a puppy you might have to only take her out of the box three times to instill the idea that if she cries, she'll get out. Then, you'll have an even tougher time breaking her of that bad habit before you can teach her the right way to act.

If that first drive is more than two hours, stop for a break. Keep the puppy on a leash and let him run around at your stopping place. The pup will certainly not know what to make of the leash, but it is important to establish and maintain control. Let the puppy wander and go to the bathroom, but restrict water. A couple hours without water won't hurt the pup and it will make the rest of the trip easier to endure for both of you.

One trick to keeping all dogs happy during car rides is to let them out as soon as you stop—even before you go to get gas or shop for a soft drink at the convenience store. Dogs seem to have to pee as soon as the vehicle stops running. Pull off to the side and let the pup take a quick run before you hit the gas pumps or the store. Your pet will thank you for it.

You want to make that first ride in the car an enjoyable experience. Be gentle with the puppy. Speak in soft tones and don't get frustrated. Remember, everything you are doing is new and scary for that little dog. You need to provide reassurance and a feeling of safety. Overly loud music,

If you reward the behavior of a dog—any behavior—you will see it repeated.

sudden stops and starts or bouts of road rage are no way to introduce a puppy to riding in a car. Keep it smooth and calm. Then, after the puppy gets out of the car, offer a little treat and lots of encouragement. The good feelings will last a long time.

Puppy's place

Once you arrive home, help your puppy explore. This is your first chance to really learn patience. While your home and yard are familiar to you, for the pup the new surroundings offer a kaleidoscope of novel smells and

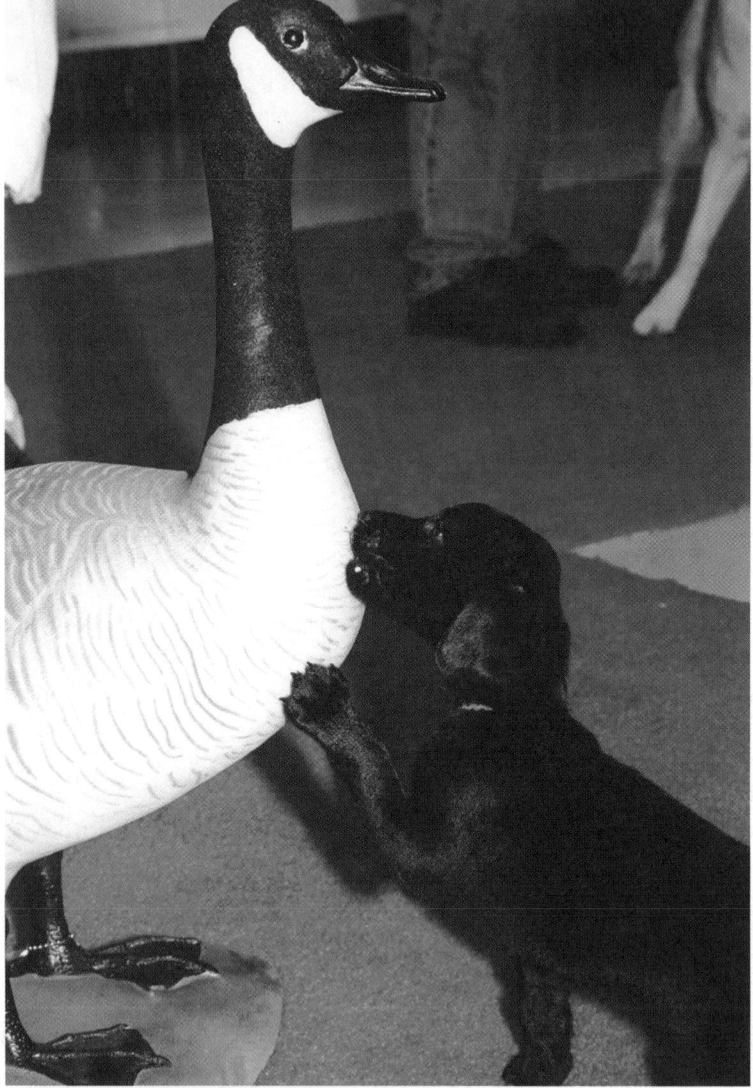

PHOTO BY JULIA JOHNSON

When your puppy arrives at his new home, let him explore—under your supervision—to help him get accustomed to his new surroundings.

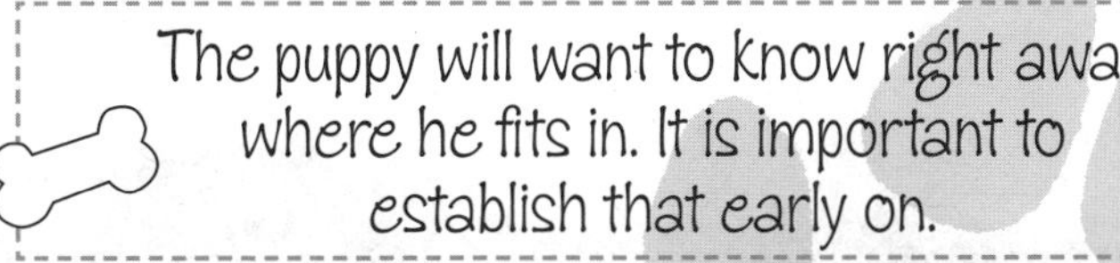

experiences. Snap on the leash and just follow the puppy around. Let her nose lead the way and you just keep up. Remember to gently enforce any boundaries like property lines and especially the curb. This is the first step in teaching the pup to stay in the yard, but more important than that, this time lets the puppy get accustomed to her new surroundings. Giving her some freedom also teaches her to be a bit bold. A bold dog, but one that responds to commands, is much better than a cowering dog the rolls on its back and urinates in the face of any new and challenging experience. Let the puppy be a dog for a little while each day. Just follow along and explore.

As for the puppy's place, take the portable kennel out of the car and haul it inside the house to an out-of-the-way corner that will become your puppy's new den. The den should be a place where the puppy can feel safe from the hustle and bustle of daily household life, but still close enough that the young dog doesn't get really lonely. Remember, the little guy has just left his littermates. He's used to being in a large active group of young dogs. Now his pack has been reduced to just you and your family. The puppy will want to know right away where he fits in. It is important to establish that early on.

Start by putting the kennel in the corner of the kitchen. That seems to be a room with plenty of activity. Every so often put the put the puppy in the kennel for about 15 minutes and go about your daily chores. The noise of the activity will let the puppy know you are nearby, but he won't be able to physically get near you. This begins to reinforce the idea that being alone is nothing to worry about. You can create a case of separation anxiety (that includes the chewing and constant barking) simply by spending every minute with your new puppy. Remember, your goal is to train this little dog so you can go off to work all day and come home to a dog that is happy and content, not one that has been running amok for hours tearing up the house and tormenting the neighbors with constant barking.

After the puppy becomes comfortable in the kennel with you nearby, move the kennel into the next room. This distance is just additional training for the dog. Soon everything will be fine whether or not you are in the room or in the house.

Try to make the puppy's new den comfortable, but not really opulent. Young dogs will chew, so don't put anything into the kennel that you can't afford to see gnawed on. That's just common sense. A simple pad and a soft blanket should be fine. Don't offer a chew toy because you might encourage nervous chewing. Your goal is to get the dog to understand that doing nothing can be a good thing.

For good early training, it is important to have the dog sleep in the kennel. Sure, puppies are cute and cuddly and you'd love to have them snuggle in bed with you, but you're asking for problems if you don't have them sleep in the

Being alone can be scary for a small puppy. It's your job to make her feel safe even when she is not physically near you.

kennel for the first couple of months. First and foremost, you'll have no control over late-night potty training. You are also teaching the dog it has to be with you all the time. If the dog whines and cries in the kennel, first try taking the dog outside to go to the bathroom. If that doesn't work, you might try playing a radio nearby the kennel; a non-confrontational talk station is a good option. If one isn't available, go with something light and soothing. If that still doesn't work, move the puppy to a different room or get some earplugs. You see, it's just like in the car. If you reward the behavior, the dog will repeat it. If the pup whines and you go into the other room to yell at the little guy, you are still rewarding the pup by showing up. If you go in the other room and talk softly, that's even worse. You are encouraging the pup to whine. Just bite the bullet and soon the dog will stop whining.

One last thing about using the kennel as the den: never, Never, NEVER, discipline the dog when it is inside the kennel, and never use the kennel as any sort of punishment. The kennel is a safe place. If the puppy runs and hides in the kennel, great. That means she has learned to find the safe place. Talk softly and patiently and wait for the puppy to come out. Don't make the kennel into a bad place through punishment or hollering or using force to get the dog out of or into the kennel.

Getting to know each other

So, how do you and pup get acquainted? Even though your mother told you to never sink to another person's level, that's just what you have to do with a new puppy. Get down on the ground and play with the puppy. Now is your chance to build that bond that will last a lifetime. This is where loyalty begins.

At first, the puppy just needs a chance to be a dog. But you are there to provide the gentle guidance a mother dog would otherwise provide.

Playing with your puppy is fun, but is also provides opportunities for you to gently assert your dominance over the little guy—a key to training success.

During early training it is essential to keep your puppy under control with a leash.

Remember the old saying: A dog will never bite when a growl will do. That's how you need to act as you get to know your puppy. Get down on the ground and let the puppy crawl over you and sniff and play. Letting the puppy get on top of you also helps to inspire boldness. This is a trait that is especially important to working and hunting dogs. If the puppy does something you don't like, do what a mother dog would do—pick the puppy up by the scruff of the neck and gently move her away from the problem area. It's very simple, but there are some tricks.

This early play-training should also be used to firmly establish who is the leader of the new pack. Put your hands on top of the puppy. That's a sign of dominance. Use constant gentle reminders to keep the puppy in line. If you turn the puppy on his back and rest the dog on your legs, you should see some squirming, but as the pup begins to trust you, it will relax. But don't overdo this; it can lead to problems with an overly submissive dog, as discussed above. A better way to establish dominance is to simply put your hand on the pup's shoulder and keep it there with gentle pressure. When the puppy resists, lean over the pup a bit and growl if you must. Establish gentle dominance early on and the training will be much easier as the dog gets older.

You should also take your new puppy places—and start right away. Proper socialization is an important element in having a well-behaved, well-adjusted dog. The more people your puppy sees and the more different situations your puppy experiences, the better off you will be in the long run. Still, there are some rules. Don't start out by taking the pup to a fancy dinner party. And don't head off to see the Fourth of July fireworks with a pup that is not accustomed to loud noises. Start by exposing the puppy to small groups of relatively mellow people. Huge crowds or overly boisterous groups will give the dog a bad feeling. When you start with small groups you are allowing the pup to build some confidence, but at the same time reinforcing the idea that you are the master and the pup should listen to you and respond to your commands no matter what types of distractions are in the general vicinity.

Continued socialization means working your way to ever-larger groups and different settings. While engaging in this type of training, remember to keep control of your puppy by keeping her on a leash. If you need to sometimes pick her up to maker her feel secure, you can do so. But there's that fine line again. Go at these things in stages.

As for teaching the pup to deal with loud noises, it's usually best to follow the example of hunting dog trainers, who must train their dogs to deal with the sound of gunshots. As with every other aspect of dog training, you have to start small and move up. To insure that your dog doesn't end up gun-shy (that's the term for a dog that's afraid of loud noises), you have to make some noise. Make small, startling noises from far away at first, and then move to louder noises close to the dog. For this you'll need a partner.

Start by playing with the puppy. In the midst of your fun time have your partner create a moderately loud bang. It can be a cap gun or banging two books together or clapping two wood blocks together. It just needs to be a fairly sharp bang. As soon as the dog notices the bang, issue some praise—maybe a little pat on the head or some friendly words—and perhaps a small treat and continue with your play as if nothing really happened. Then have your assistant move closer and do it again. Continue this over several days. Make the loud noises as the dog is fed, do what you need to do to get the dog used to hearing the noise and not associating anything bad with the sound. On the contrary, if the puppy associates the sound with something good, your dog might just perk up at the sound of a loud noise. In fact, most hunting retrievers tense up and become very alert at the sound of gunfire, because they associate the shot with a chance to make a retrieve.

All of this socialization lets the puppy learn his place in the new pack. Through all of these new experiences the common denominator is your control over the pup. You are the leader of the pack. You show what is acceptable behavior and you show that new experiences are really nothing to be afraid of. These little trips out into the world need not be long and drawn out. Spend 15 minutes in the corner of the local park walking the pup and watching the children play. Go to a softball game for a couple of innings. You don't want to overwhelm the puppy, but you must get the little guy out there to see new things.

Establish gentle dominance early on and the training will be much easier as the dog gets older.

Feeding time

At first, puppies do two things. One of them is eat. The other is what happens after they're done eating. How, when and what you feed your puppy are all very important. I'll repeat some of this in the upcoming chapter on housebreaking, but here we'll focus more on what to feed, how it's done and a little bit on when to feed. Nutrition for the puppy's first year is of utmost importance. It can have a huge impact on the longevity and health of your dog. The better the nutrition during the first year, the healthier your dog will be throughout its life.

Dr. Arleigh Reynolds is veterinarian specializing in nutritional studies with Purina and his suggestions for healthy puppies start even before the new litter is conceived.

"You have to start with a healthy mom," Reynolds says. "Not too thin and not too fat. When it's time to breed her, you should start feeding her a good quality puppy food or a performance food."

You may not have much control over what the breeder feeds his or her dogs during pregnancy, but at least you can ask and then make a better-informed decision about buying a puppy. And if you plan to raise a litter of your own, you'll know the nutritional needs and how they relate to raising healthy puppies.

During pregnancy, which lasts only about 60 days for most dogs, Reynolds said that starting with the fifth week of the pregnancy the expectant mom should get about 10 percent more food per week, until the dog is eating 1.5 times her normal meals. These will have to be spaced out over several small meals because the puppies growing inside her will not allow her to eat much at each meal.

This nursing mother needs an incredible amount of feed to maintain a healthy milk supply—approximately 50 percent more food than normal per puppy.

After delivery, the key time in nutritional terms is three to six weeks after the birth of the pups. This is the peak milk production period for the mother. To keep the pups healthy, she will need a 50 percent increase in food FOR EACH PUPPY. Reynolds stressed this fact because many people underfeed nursing dogs—simply because they don't know how much food it takes to produce that much high-quality milk. So, a litter of eight puppies means the nursing mom will get four times her normal food during the three to six weeks after the puppies are born. This amount of food will obviously have to be offered in several small meals throughout the day.

Reynolds also says that puppies should be wormed every three weeks from the time the dogs reach 3 weeks of age until they are 15 weeks old.

"Fully 95 percent of all puppies have worms and those worms can sometimes kill a puppy before the eggs show up in the stool," Reynolds said. "Some puppies can get a lethal dose of hookworms through the milk while suckling."

You can begin weaning pups at about 3 weeks of age by soaking food in warm water and letting them walk in it, lick it and learn to eat it. As the pups are being weaned, you can cut the amount of food to the mother, but still keep giving her lots of water.

For a new puppy in your house, you should be feeding the pup three meals for about the first six months, following the instructions on the package and the recommendations of your vet. Reynolds said puppies should eat about twice the amount of food per pound of body weight as an adult dog during the first six months. Then from six to nine months, they should eat 1.5 times that of an adult dog per pound of body weight.

"Everyone wants a magic formula for feeding a dog," said Reynolds. "It is more important to feed to the right body condition. If anything, it is better to slightly underfeed a puppy than to overfeed."

Reynolds says you should be able to feel the tops of the spine, at least two ribs and tips of the hips. "You don't want rounded hips," he said.

Dogs that put on too much weigh early in life can suffer serious bone diseases later on. One of the most important times to keep a close eye on feeding is when pups are between 4 and 8 months old. At that time, large-breed dogs should not gain more than 3 to 3.5 pounds per week. Weigh your puppy regularly and keep their weight gain under control.

"If you feed properly during this time you can cut the likelihood of hip problems by threefold," said Reynolds.

The way you feed your dog can be as important as the amount and type of food you feed. In the wild, the leader of the pack decides when other members of the pack will eat. Exercising your authority as the leader of the

The better the nutrition during the first year, the healthier your dog will be throughout its life.

This puppy needs good nutrition to help him along in life. Puppies need about twice the amount of food per body weight as adult dogs.

pack will help show your puppy you mean business. Get a bowl of food, grab the pup by the collar and hold on. Set the food down and hold the pup back. The best thing is to talk softly and encourage the puppy to calm down. Then, when the puppy is calm, allow her to go eat. Don't be rough. Don't be loud. Just be persistent. This might take five or 10 minutes at mealtime, but it will pay big dividends later on, especially if you have a big dog. Do you really want a 90-pound German Shepherd jumping around excitedly trying to get at the bowl of food you are holding? If you restrain that 20-pound puppy and train her that she only eats when you say so, you won't have to worry later on.

Finally, there is the issue of timing. Your dog needs to eat when you say so. This will be of paramount importance during housebreaking, so start now. After you allow the puppy to start eating, leave the food out for just 20 minutes. If the pup hasn't eaten all the food in 20 minutes, take what remains away and offer no other food until the next scheduled feeding. After the dog misses a couple of meals, your problems with a finicky eater will be gone. And remember what Dr. Reynolds said: It's better to underfeed a little than to overfeed.

Go with the flow

Now, you are home with your new puppy. You've made that first drive, established a safe haven for the young dog, begun the all-important work of socialization and gotten a primer on food and feeding. So, what's next?

By being patient, calm and persistent with your puppy you can end up with a well-trained young dog like this one.

You name it. That's what's next. The first several weeks with a new puppy in the home will be unpredictable. Establishing a routine will help, but puppies are, well, puppies. Things will get chewed. There will be accidents on the floor. If you are not careful, some things may get knocked over and broken. The key is to not get upset and lose your cool. Doing so is completely counterproductive. Getting frustrated, yelling and hitting a puppy are not training techniques. You won't get what you want by being loud and forceful. You will get what you want by being patient, calm and persistent. Persistence, to the point of being repetitive, is the basis of all good dog training. The goal is to show the dog what you actions you want and to offer praise for the correct actions. Do this several times and the dog will get into the habit of doing what you want. Be ready for a few setbacks. Such setbacks are not the end of the world, they are just bumps on the road to a well-trained young dog. Getting a dog to do what you want is not difficult and it should never be hard on the dog. Keep that in mind and the information in the next few chapters will fall right into place.

Chapter Four

Housebreaking: Easier Than You Think

First things first: If your puppy is going to live indoors, you must make sure the animal is completely housebroken. That is, you must train your dog to defecate and urinate only outdoors and, better yet, only in a certain spot outdoors. Training your puppy to go on newspaper is not a substitute for housebreaking and can actually lead to problems down the road. Use paper as an emergency measure; your goal is to teach the dog to control its bodily functions until it is outside. You can do it! It's really not all that difficult.

> Dogs can be housebroken because they are den-dwelling animals. They love to sleep in a warm, cozy den. Everything else happens outside the den.

Most people buy puppies when the little fur balls are about 8 weeks old. This is a very important time for the dog psychologically. Not only is the pup in the middle of learning human socialization skills, but the animal is also very delicate when it comes to responding to fear. Harsh discipline at such an early age should be avoided or it may impact the dog for months or years to come. So, you can start housebreaking the day you bring your pup home, but go easy on the discipline. Dogs can be housebroken because they are, at their most basic level, den-dwelling animals. As such, they love to sleep in a warm, cozy den. Everything else happens outside the den. Dogs eat, socialize, mate and relieve themselves away from their dens. Dogs also love schedules and they fall very nicely into routines. These daily duties provide structure, security and seem to give puppies a sense of confidence in understanding their environment. Sticking to a schedule for a long enough time can make the actions of the animal almost automatic. So that's where to start the housebreaking

The most important aspect of house training is the schedule. Puppies typically have a bowel movement just a few minutes after eating. With some puppies the interval is up to 20 minutes, but knowing that soon after your pup eats it will have to go is a great place for you start your schedule. This means you should plan your day and your training around regular feedings. And I do mean regular. If you are not maintaining the schedule of a German subway conductor, your housebreaking will suffer and you'll have the carpet cleaning bills to prove it. So, lay in an ample supply of good-quality dog food, feed amounts according to the label instructions or your veterinarian's recommendations and establish a schedule that you are willing and able to maintain for several months. Don't panic, the housebreaking should only take a week or two, but maintaining the schedule will insure you don't have to deal with any accidents from your young dog.

Always have the puppy relieve himself in the same general area. This helps to reinforce the housebreaking schedule.

Control the Input and the Output

If you control not only what, but when, something goes into your puppy, you will have a big advantage in knowing when something will come out of your puppy. Present the food on schedule and take it away after about 20 minutes. This encourages the puppy to eat when you want. Soon after that, he'll have to go.

The schedule

From 8 weeks to 3 months of age, you'll be feeding your puppy four times a day with meals in the morning, at noon, late afternoon and an hour before bedtime. The hour before bed allows the dog to digest the food and relieve himself prior to sleeping. Once the puppy passes 3 months you can shift to a morning, after work and before bed feeding schedule. One of the keys to success will be to always take the young dog out soon after eating and drinking and encourage the dog to "do its business" outside. You can't forget. You can't have something else to do…this is the time the training happens. You need to control this schedule, especially early on.

Food and water

Serve recommended portions of food, along with a bowl of water, at the appointed times, and make both available for only 20 to 25 minutes. Take away the bowls after 25 minutes, even if the puppy hasn't finished eating all of the food. This will encourage the puppy to eat right away and allow you to stay on your schedule. There should be no free access to food at this time. I don't believe free-feeding is a great idea anyway, but it is especially bad when you are trying to housebreak a dog. And, don't go changing dog food brands in the middle of the housebreaking. A new kind of dog food can trigger diarrhea. Not only does that make it even harder for a young dog to "hold it," but the clean up is not much fun either.

The crate

Some call it a "den" or a dog box or a portable kennel. I call it a crate. Used in conjunction with the schedule, the crate will allow you to quickly housebreak the dog with very few accidents. Do not be cheap about dog crates. Get a good one and get one that is right for your dog's current size. Don't buy one that's too big and wait for your dog to grow into it. Buy the right size, and as the puppy grows, buy bigger crates. You might end up with three by the time the dog is full grown, but the headaches you'll save will be worth the cost.

Embrace the crate, because it allows you to use thousands of years of dog instincts to your advantage.

Love the Crate

Quite simply, crate training is THE best way to quickly and efficiently housebreak a puppy. The two most important elements are the schedule and the crate. In order for the crate to work as it should, it has to be an enjoyable place. Nothing bad can ever happen to a puppy in a crate…no corrections…no punishment…nothing. The crate has to be a place in which the puppy is comfortable and at ease.

Embrace the crate, because it allows you to use thousands of years of dog instincts to your advantage. The idea of the crate is that a dog will not soil his den. That's why dogs are so easy to housebreak. You can confine the dog in a crate while you are controlling the supply of food and water to teach the dog that relieving himself is something done only outside. The double bonus of using a crate is that during the training the dog also learns to get over any separation anxiety. The best thing you can do for a young dog is allow the animal to be alone sometimes. Then, when you are gone to work you won't have to deal with a lot of barking, chewing or other bad behavior—but that's for another chapter.

Another thing about crates: Get the right size. If you bought a beautiful

Controlling the puppy's food is the only way to effectively housebreak a young dog. Don't give the puppy the chance to have an accident.

yellow Lab puppy that will one day grow to be 75 pounds you still need a small crate to start the housebreaking, and then you will get progressively larger ones as the dog grows. A crate of the proper size will allow the dog to stand and turn around, but not much more. That's what you want. You put a 10-pound puppy into a crate for a 75-pound dog and the puppy will have enough room to think he can go to the bathroom in one corner. If that happens, even once, your training has to start all over. If the dog poops in *his* house, he will certainly poop in *yours*.

Every once in a while I will hear a comment about, "That poor dog doesn't have enough room in there." Don't fall for the sentimental stuff. If the dog has enough room to lie down and wait for you to open the door, the crate is great. I have a prime example: I take my dogs to work with me and they sleep in portable kennels on a flatbed trailer in the parking lot. At 10 a.m., noon and 3 p.m. I go outside to exercise and train the dogs. Invariably some well-meaning dog owner will catch me in the hall and complain that it's not fair that I leave my dogs in those "tiny boxes all day."

I have a great response. First I say, "If I left those dogs home in their kennels they would curl up in their dog houses, which are exactly the same size as the portable kennels, and pretty much sleep until I get home." That usually stops the do-gooder in mid-thought. Then I add, "And, when the dogs are here, I get to play with them three times per day. When was the last time you played with your dog three times in a single day?"

End of discussion.

The point of all this is that a smaller crate will serve your needs. When the puppy outgrows it, buy a bigger one. The crates are inexpensive and for all the good they do, you can afford to have an extra one around. Who knows when you'll buy that next puppy?

The plan

So you have the food and water, the crate and a general idea that you should follow a schedule. It will be tough for the first month, but by the time the puppy is 3 months old, she should have the muscle control to hold it for fairly long periods of time. That first month, expect some "accidents" and don't worry about discipline. The idea is to teach acceptable behavior, not change "bad" habits. For that first month, come home over lunch or hire a neighbor to take the puppy out and generally keep cleaning up while you work on the basics of feeding the pup and taking him out a few minutes after he eats and drinks. At 3 months of age, you can start the real training. It will go something like this if you work during the day:

While you are housebreaking the puppy, there should be no playtime outside. You are trying to convince the dog that outside is the place for her to relieve herself.

The Schedule is Everything

You must establish a schedule and you must be able to maintain that schedule for at least three weeks. If your dog is going to live inside, these are most important three weeks of your life. Make it work. Do it right and you never have to worry about housebreaking again.

6:30 a.m.	Wake up and take pup out immediately
6:45 to 7 a.m.	Playtime for pup (with some supervision)
7 a.m.	Food and water
7:25 a.m.	Go out
7:45 a.m.	Into the crate
5:30 or 6 p.m.	Return from work and take pup out immediately
6:15 p.m.	Playtime
6:30 p.m.	Into the crate
7:35 p.m.	Food and water
8 p.m.	Go out
8:15 to 8:30	Playtime
8:30 p.m.	Into the crate
10:30 p.m.	Food and water
10:55 p.m.	Go out (be patient now and make sure the dog relieves himself)
11:30 p.m.	Into the crate for the night

During these playtime breaks you should be working on the basic commands, especially "Sit." This is a great time to start some short training sessions. But keep them very short and play with the dog some, too.

During housebreaking, time outside should be devoted to the puppy relieving itself. Playtime will only confuse the training process.

While you are housebreaking the puppy, you should only take her out to urinate and defecate. There should be no playtime outside. You are trying to convince the dog that outside is the place for her to relieve herself. It's also best to take the dog to the same general area, each time you go out. That way the scent from previous outings will encourage the dog to go. Also, if the dog doesn't relieve himself within about 10 minutes after you go outside, take him back in and put him in the crate for about 10 minutes (but keep an eye on him). After a short time in the crate take the puppy out again. Also, remember to praise the puppy intensely when she does her business in the right spot.

It should only take 10 to 12 days to housebreak a 3-month-old pup with this method. Just remember to maintain the schedule, praise the positive work and clean the "accidents" thoroughly.

Urban dwellers

Dogs living in the city have it a bit tougher than their country cousins. Plan your feeding and outside schedule to include "travel time" down the hall, into the elevator and out the door. Also, plan to carry your pup all the way outside, especially first thing in the morning and after returning from

Urban dwellers have a tougher time with housebreaking. Make sure your puppy is on a leash at all times, encourage using the curb rather than the sidewalk, and always clean up after your dog.

work, during the early stages of the training. This will prevent accidents on the way to the curb. Once outside, make sure your dog is on a leash at all times. You can use the leash to guide the puppy to the curb and encourage her to relieve herself there, instead of in the middle of the sidewalk.

Another tip for city residents: Make the dog go close to the door of your apartment building. This will insure that you don't have walk around the block if it is raining or snowing.

Crate time is very important for city dogs. Keeping the dog in the crate, and showing no attention to whining or whimpering, will teach your dog that it's okay to be in the crate alone. You won't have to hear your neighbors complain that your lovable little puppy barked or howled all day.

Finally, make sure you clean up after your dog.

What if it just doesn't work?

Effective housebreaking is based on the idea that you have a healthy dog. Most puppies should be able to hold it through the night by the time they are 15 weeks old if you let them go out just before bed, and restrict water during the night. Some common dog maladies will throw your housebreaking program into disarray. Watch out for things like bladder infections that make it tough for a dog to hold urine for any length of time. Problems with digestion can show up as loose, runny stools. These are typically caused by changes in the diet or because your dog was fed table scraps. Pay attention, however distasteful you find it, to the consistency of your dog's stools. If you haven't changed the dog's food and know there are no table scraps in the animal's diet, call your vet if your dog suffers from frequent, loose stools.

There are plenty of other symptoms to pay attention to, as well. If your dog is constipated or appears to be straining during defecation, contact your vet. Changes in eating or drinking habits or bad breath can also be a signal that something is not right. An acquaintance of mine decided to take his dog to the vet to do something about the dog's serious case of bad breath. The doctor found a 3-inch stick lodged in the roof of the dog's mouth between teeth! Vomiting, blood in the urine or stool or a temperature of more than 102 degrees F are all reasons to have your dog checked by a vet right away.

Jealousy

Believe it or not, jealousy can play a role in housebreaking. More precisely, it can be the cause of "accidents" or slip-ups in an otherwise well-trained dog. If your housebroken dog suddenly starts having accidents in the house,

Effective housebreaking is based on the idea that you have a healthy dog. Some common dog maladies will throw your housebreaking program into disarray.

check to see if the accidents coincide with the arrival of anything that is directly competing with the dog for your attention. Another dog or a new puppy would be obvious, but realize, too, that a new baby can cause a dog to start wondering where he fits into the scheme of things.

To remedy slip-ups or accidents, maintain your schedule religiously and pay attention where you give your attention. If you are falling all over yourself to care for a new baby and you forget about the dog, it's only natural for the dog to be confused about where it fits into the "pack." Remember to include the dog in your activities with the baby and continue to encourage good behavior through praise.

If it's a new dog causing the problems, again, get back to strict schedule. The easiest way is to include both dogs during the training of the newcomer. This will not only get the dogs used to being around one another, but it will also allow the veteran to "show" the new arrival how things work. The new dog will instinctively watch the actions of the other dog and follow suit as it works to find its place in the pack. This is also a time for careful supervision, especially during joint playtime, because there are bound to be some dominance issues raised, especially if the dogs are close to the same size.

New house, new training

You may also run into trouble with your dog if you move to a new house or apartment. Be prepared to get back to some serious scheduling and crate training, especially if you are moving from a quiet area to someplace noisy. Moving to a new house means you are upsetting the familiarity your dog has with its current schedule. It can take a while to get things back on track. Be prepared for a few setbacks and plan accordingly. As always, consistency and diligence will be the keys to working through any problems.

PHOTO BY JULIA JOHNSON

Older dogs can sometimes disrupt the housebreaking process, or they might have their own jealousy-inspired "accidents." Include all your dogs in the new puppy's training to keep peace in the house.

Chapter Five

Basic Training: For You and Your Puppy

People often ask, "At what age should I start training my puppy?" This question seems to just pop out, as if training is some sort of program with a set schedule and finite goals. On the contrary, dog training is an ongoing process that begins the day your puppy is born.

Good training in the first year of life gives you a dog like this. No running around like mad and no jumping—the model of good behavior.

If you have done all your homework and selected a reputable breeder, the socialization of your puppy very likely began within a few minutes of its birth. All puppies should be handled almost immediately. They need to be dried, inspected and cuddled and should be removed from the whelping area and kept warm as the mother delivers the next pup. This early activity starts the process of showing the pup that it must submit to the wishes of humans. There's nothing defined or directed about this activity, but such handling is very important in getting the young dog acclimated to the life it will soon lead.

Most puppies arrive at their new homes at about 8 weeks of age and the "training" should begin that day. By training, I mean to say that the new owner should immediately establish a routine. Feeding, playing, quiet time and potty breaks should all revolve around a schedule that serves to show the puppy that you are calling the shots. All of these activities really qualify as training. Still, there is no need to be harsh or to attempt to correct a puppy's behavior at this stage—simply establish a routine, spend plenty of time with the dog and do simple things to make the dog understand that you are the boss. Some of those things include holding the dog back from the food dish for a few seconds or a minute, rubbing on its shoulders and neck area (sign of dominance) and picking the puppy up and holding the animal until it stops squirming. All these things show the dog you are in control, and this will help you later on.

Once the puppy is about 3 months old (remember that is about one month after you get the dog) you can start to work on things like housebreaking and simple obedience commands. With housebreaking, the key is to keep a strict schedule and control food and water at all times until the dog is completely housebroken.

Simple obedience commands like "Sit" and "Come" can be taught at this early age, but you must remain patient and kind as you repeatedly show the

Building Blocks of Training

This will be the biggest section of the book because I'll describe in detail what you'll be doing to train your puppy. Throughout this section, I refer to training as building blocks of information. The more your puppy learns, the more it will be able to learn and each previous session will prepare you and the puppy for the next step. Have you ever watched in awe as a dog owner simply called their dog and it ran over to sit by that person's side? If you counted all the things a puppy must learn to complete that simple operation, you might be startled. But, all things can be taught using short and effective training sessions. And that's where we start.

"But I'm so cute." Don't ever give in. Require compliance with your commands. Being tough will be better for your pup in the long run.

A good collar is a great asset when training. Get the right size.

dog what you want it to do after you issue the command. That's why we try to work in 15-minute training sessions. Not only is it easier for you to find 15 minutes a couple of times per day, but in that short span of time you'll likely remain patient and calm during the entire training session. If you lose your cool, training pretty much stops. Before and after your dedicated 15-minute training session you should continue handling the puppy and gently showing the animal your dominance. This makes the dog more willing to comply with your commands.

After a couple of weeks of basic obedience training you should begin taking your pup out in public, so the dog learns how to act around other people. This requires real patience on your part. During the first few trips to crowded parks or busy sidewalks, your puppy will undoubtedly ignore your commands completely. Keep the dog on the leash and simply reinforce the commands. Above all, stay calm. Yelling at, or worse yet, hitting the dog will only prove to the dog that crowds and other people are something to be afraid of. In doing so, you might never be able to easily control your dog in such situations.

You'll also want to have a helper or other family member start giving some of the basic commands. This helps the young dog to understand that commands must be obeyed, no matter who gives them.

In all cases, keep your training time short in duration and finish the training when the dog has succeeded in completing a task. Your goal is to create that 15-minute block of time in which the dog succeeds at the tasks you've set out to accomplish. Ending on a positive note reinforces the idea to the dog that the training sessions are something to look forward to. If you start training early and remain consistent, your progress will be amazing. It's never too early to start training your pup.

The key to solid training in a short time is to get the puppy's attention, reinforce simple commands quickly, then quit before the puppy gets sick of you and tunes you out.

Leash training fundamentals

Complete leash training is a gradual process. However, the fundamentals of leash training are an essential part of basic puppy training. Begin by having your puppy wear a collar. She may resist this at first, but do not give in; for the safety of your puppy this is one rule that must not be broken. Once your puppy is used to the collar, begin letting her drag her leash around the house for 15 minutes at a time, under your supervision. When it's potty time, guide the puppy to her potty place on her leash. Get her used to walking on your left side by simply placing her there each and every time you take her outside. Most puppies learn to love their leash since it's a signal they're going outside—and puppies love to explore!

The 15-minute miracle

Two of the most important aspects of puppy training are how you organize it and where you conduct it. Putting a little forethought into your training sessions will insure that you get the most benefit and fun out of the time you spend working with your puppy. Our goal here is to train by devoting 15-minute blocks of time to your dog. If you are really enthusiastic, you can create several 15-minute sessions, but that's not required. Everyone is busy. Everyone has a life beyond the puppy. If you train, really train, for 15

Puppies of all breeds can be energetic and feisty. Be firm, but patient with them.

Keep the training sessions short, and you will keep the puppy's attention.

minutes each day, your puppy will be fine. This type of training works because several short training sessions are better than one long one. You can even go a step further by breaking your 15-minute sessions into five-minute segments with a minute or two of playtime tucked between each training operation.

This all works because puppies, especially young puppies, have really short attention spans. The key to solid training in a short time is to get the puppy's attention, reinforce simple commands quickly, then quit before the puppy gets sick of you and tunes you out. After a short break for some play or a walk, you can get right back to the training while the last lesson is still fresh in the puppy's head. By keeping the training segments short, your puppy not only stays interested, it doesn't get physically tired, either. A puppy that is fresh and alert takes to training better than one that just wants to lie down and rest.

Another argument for keeping the training sessions short is that you'll be more likely to keep at it. Let's face it; we all have demands on our time. If you thought for a minute that you'd need two solid hours each day to train your puppy, what would happen to your puppy? But knowing that you only need 15 minutes makes it more likely that you'll get out there and actually engage in real training. So, really, everybody wins when the training sessions are kept short.

Finally, there's no rule that says the only time you spend with your puppy must be training time. To have a healthy, happy puppy, you need to have bonding time as well. There are times when a puppy just needs to get out and explore, romp around and have a great time. The cool thing about this is you can make these times into mini-training sessions and the puppy won't know the difference; she'll just like the fact that she's getting out and doing something. If, in the middle of one of your puppy "play" sessions, you pop in a command (and reinforce it), your dog will learn quickly that commands must be obeyed no matter what is going on.

Training the trainer: What are YOU doing?

Before you can train a puppy, you have to have some idea of what you are doing. Puppies are sponges. Do the same thing and demand the same result enough times and your puppy will learn to do what you say. It is that simple. So don't shake your head and say, "I just don't have the time." You see, the first thing you need to know about puppy training is that it doesn't take a lot of time. In fact, your puppy will get more out of your training sessions if you keep them short.

If you're one of those people who thinks having a well-trained puppy means hour upon hour of diligent training, think again. You can train your puppy in 15 minutes a day. You just need to know how. Luckily there's no mystery involved. There's nothing truly amazing about the techniques of professional dog trainers. They issue simple commands and they repeat the sequence until the puppy's reaction to the command becomes second nature. Remember, puppies are sponges.

To train your puppy in basic obedience, all you really need to do is focus on the training for a few minutes each day. During that time you'll teach some basic commands and repeat them until the puppy understands how you want things done. It's like building with blocks. Each block is the foundation

> There is nothing difficult about training a puppy. What can be difficult is *learning* to train a puppy.

Voice commands—in this case a good firm "No"—help to reinforce what you are training.

for the next step. Follow the simple training tips presented in this book and you will build a foundation of basic skills that will make your pet a joy to be around.

There is nothing difficult about training a puppy. What can be difficult is *learning* to train a puppy. It's not that the techniques are so tough or the commands so difficult to master, it's just that while you are training your puppy you have to stop thinking in human terms. Puppies don't use logic or reason, they just respond. It's a simple case of action and reaction, and the puppy learns through repetition.

It would be easy to say, "You have to think like a puppy." But we humans don't really know how puppies think. All I really know is that puppies want food and attention and something to play with. A little kid is a really good thing for a puppy to play with, but if you don't have one, don't worry—your puppy will be fine. As far as how puppies think, we only know how puppies *react* to what we do. They are members of a pack and respond instinctively to every situation. We can observe changes in their posture and demeanor as we change the tone of our voice, our posture, our actions or even the looks on our faces. This is where puppy training really starts. It is about paying attention to how the puppy reacts to what you do and say. Once you start to notice these things, then you can begin to modify a puppy's behavior by showing the animal what you expect, giving a simple command, forcing the puppy to comply and repeating the sequence (notice I said repeating the sequence—not the command—more on that later) until the action—actually the reaction to the command—becomes automatic.

But here is the rub with puppies: It is very easy to go too far. Early training should be brief and fun. It should never be hostile or loud. And if you are getting frustrated, stop. Just stop and let the puppy play or sleep or curl up next to you in the easy chair. There is a possibility that, if you get angry, you could scare the puppy so badly that it will take months for the puppy to trust you again. Don't go that far. Go easy. Be persistent and firm, not rough or loud.

Patience, patience, patience

Therefore, the first step in training a puppy is to train the trainer. This begins and ends with patience. Patience will be your master while you are trying to teach your puppy. Lose your patience and your training session will end. That is to say, if you are impatient or irritable, the training you *hope* to

This is the right place to start training a puppy to come. First teach the pup to sit. Then move on from there.

This is a puppy ready to listen and learn. When teaching a dog to come, always make responding to the command a good thing.

provide will stop, even if you double the amount of time. On top of that, if you become impatient, your puppy may be learning things you don't want him to learn. Then, you will have to backtrack and remedy those "bad habits" before you move ahead teaching the things that are really important.

Lost patience typically shows up as some sort of aggressive frustration on the part of the puppy trainer. There are as many different manifestations of lost patience as there are puppy owners in the world. The worst of these include shouting at, hitting, kicking or using the leash to beat your puppy. Don't let these ever happen. Before your frustration reaches the point that you feel like you will become violent (I consider shouting violent because it teaches the puppy nothing but to fear you) stop your training session and take a break. That break may last as long as a day, but don't let the challenges inherent in teaching an animal push you to the point of doing something that will: 1) Be abusive to the animal; 2) Reduce the effectiveness of your training session; and 3) Make you consider, even for a minute, that your puppy can't be trained in basic obedience.

If you are like most puppy owners, you will never enter a competition of any sort with your pet. But all of us want our puppies to come, sit and lie down on command. We don't want the puppy barking all night long and we would enjoy walking the puppy much more if we weren't getting dragged all over town by a hyperactive canine. This book is not about creating an

If the puppy fails, be gentle but firm. Don't let her get away with anything just because she's cute.

expert hunting retriever, training an agility champion or teaching your family pet to track down missing fugitives, but you can bet all the puppies that eventually fill those specialist roles first mastered the basic skills that will be presented here.

Like I said before, puppies don't think like you and me. And when it comes to training, I don't know that I care if a puppy reasons at all. What I want is for the puppy to *react* to the stimuli that I present. If I call, I want the puppy to at least look at me. I can compel the dog to come as part of the training, but first I want to know the animal is paying attention to me and understands I am the master. Making the puppy look my way is not much of a trick. I can just blow a whistle. But it's that interest I want. First we get the interest, then we quickly encourage the response.

It is also important to understand that training this puppy is for you. It is a personal thing only administered to suit your desires. To put it simply, you want the puppy to do what you want the puppy to do. The key to getting the puppy to do what you want is patience. Combine that with a little bit of repetition and your puppy will respond to the training.

Training through repetition is where most people get tangled up believing, "I don't have time to train a puppy." That statement is simply not true. You have the time because dogs have wonderful memories for routines. Puppies have very short attention spans—lots of things distract them—but that's actually an advantage because we want to keep the training sessions short. You need simply need to be patient, repetitive and consistent. If you lose your cool, especially if you do it repeatedly, all the puppy is going to remember is, "That person yells a lot and hits me. I'm not going over there." On the other hand, if you give the same command and consistently demand the same reaction to that command, then praise the success and consistently correct the failures, your puppy will understand and will soon respond without hesitation.

Puppies don't reason. Rover doesn't know that he got hit because he failed to respond to the first command. Rover only knows that he got hit. So don't hit. It's counter-productive.

You need to be firm, but not violent. One of the best ways to remember this is to remember that the puppy is supposed to be your friend. The puppy is supposed to bring you happiness. Remember that in most cases of "disobedience" the puppy is just being a puppy. The animal is simply acting on the instincts that make it a puppy and your training has not yet convinced the puppy to ignore instinct and listen to you.

Know your puppy?

Puppies, at the very core of their being, need to live in a pack. Realize also that you have just removed your puppy from a big group of other puppies. Things are changing fast for the little dog. Puppies stay with their litter for about eight weeks. In that time, they learn the basic social order of dogs. They become part of a pack. Then, we take them away to a new home. Still, the pack mentality is woven so deeply into the inner workings of every puppy that there is no hope of trying to overcome it, change it or ignore it. Those of us who hope to train puppies have to understand what the pack means to the puppy and use that knowledge to help in training.

For wild dogs, the pack provided everything: training and discipline, fellowship and food. In domestic dogs, we've removed the animal from traditional communal living and we demand that it act in accordance with our rules. We are expecting a lot from our 3-month-old dog. The result is

The pack mentality is woven so deeply into the inner workings of every puppy that there is no hope of trying to overcome it, change it or ignore it.

Playtime and training should be rolled into one. Training should be fun and playtime should teach something.

that we can best train them by providing some semblance of life in a pack. You must take the place of the pack.

The great thing about this is that your puppy makes it easy. Your puppy wants nothing more than to be with you. When you leave for the day, the puppy, unless it is suffering from acute separation anxiety, simply lies down and waits for you to come back. When you come back, the puppy is happy again, because it knows it is part of the pack.

The very first thing you have to teach the puppy is its place in the pack. As the puppy's trainer you must assume the role of the leader. In a real pack there is a strict social hierarchy. The leader makes the rules, allows other members to eat and establishes crude discipline. You can take on all these responsibilities. Once the puppy understands that you are the leader, training comes very easily. This is because members of the pack very rarely challenge the leader once the hierarchy has been established. A young wolf may step up to lead the pack once the alpha wolf starts to age, because order is established through dominance. You need to be the dominant member of the pack in order to train your puppy. The tricky part is to show the puppy you are in charge without breaking the animal's spirit. This is not as difficult as it sounds. There are four steps—and remember the old saying: A dog won't bite when a growl will do. You don't want to scare the puppy to the point that it's afraid to move or rolls over and wets. Use just enough dominant behavior to get the little guy's attention.

The Look: This is the look Mom gave you as a child when you were acting up in public—that direct, piercing stare. It is especially powerful when used against puppies. It is a challenge, and puppies know they are smaller and less powerful than you. Young dogs are especially intimidated by this type of activity and will often drop their head and assume a submissive posture immediately. That's when you both know you are in charge.

The Lean: The next step in showing who's the boss is simply moving in close and leaning over the puppy. This is an even more direct challenge than staring at the puppy. This works especially good on a puppy that won't sit. Just move in close and look down at the puppy. You'll get almost instant compliance.

The Touch: In wolf packs the dominant wolf will approach other wolves and place his muzzle or paws on the shoulder of a subordinate animal. When you praise your puppy and pet the animal on the shoulder, you are doing the same thing. This is a great way provide encouragement while at the same time show you are in command. Use this technique often and your training will be very easy.

Grabbing the throat: This is the only dominance behavior that requires you to make noise. Typically, this option is used for older, untrained dogs that are very used to having their own way. If you have a puppy that is particularly stubborn and refuses to accept your position at the leader of the pack, you have to go for the throat. There is no intent to harm the puppy. You are simply communicating in a manner that the puppy, through tens of thousands of years of evolution, will understand completely. Kneel down and let the puppy come in close. Get one hand on the collar and pull the puppy to the ground as you roll the animal to his back. Grab the throat and growl loudly. As you let the puppy up lean over him and keep one hand firmly on the puppy's shoulders. You should only have to do this a few times and the animal will get the message.

Other important aspects of establishing and maintaining dominance include taking control, keeping control and giving commands.

Not only does this make the puppy feel good, it reinforces your control of the puppy. This is a submissive posture and the puppy knows you are the boss.

Don't let the puppy even think he controls the food. Establish your dominance by making him wait until you say it's okay to eat.

Taking control means just that: You must immediately establish a leadership role with the puppy. The puppy is small and you are big. You can simply pick up the puppy if you have to and there is no danger of the little critter yanking your arm out of joint when you attach the leash.

Everything you do should reinforce to the puppy that you are in control of the pack. When you bring out the puppy's food, make the puppy sit and wait to eat until you say it's okay to do so. When you open the door to take the puppy out for a walk or a training session, make the puppy wait so that you can step outside first. In the wild, the dominant dog also decides when it's time to play and when the pack will get up and move to a new location. You need to fill all those roles to be an effective trainer. All of this is pack behavior and you are constantly showing your dominance in subtle ways.

The correction

In the training portions of this book you'll see the term "correction." Most of the time I'll use this term when I want you to apply a short tug on the leash to remind the puppy that you are in charge and whatever the puppy just did was not appropriate. A correction is quick and immediate. Never yank hard on the leash. Never lift the puppy off the ground by the leash. Never whip the puppy with the leash. Just give a short tug. If you need to add strength to the correction, say, "No" in a firm voice as you give the correction. Combine that with staring at the puppy or leaning over the animal and you'll be amazed at how quickly a puppy comes to figure out that if he does what he is asked, no correction is needed.

The thing to remember about a correction is that that it must be immediate. A puppy doesn't remember what he did 10 minutes ago. The sequence must be swift: infraction/correction. Then, immediately continue training. Tugging the leash five times won't do any more good than tugging it

Train the puppy to stand still as you attach the leash to the collar.

Notice how the puppy is looking up to its master for a cue. That's a good thing.

once. If a tug doesn't work, add a look. Then add a lean. Then, finally, pick the puppy up. He'll get the message.

The other side of the correction coin is praise. Use it often, but make it meaningful.

Meaningful praise is applied just like a correction: immediately. As soon as the puppy does something you like, smile and say, "Good dog." This is a great time, too, to rub the puppy on the shoulders, thus explaining to the animal that the dominant member of the pack approves of the action.

Praise can be anything from a simple expression to a syrupy and congratulatory "Goooood puppy. What a good puppy. Yeah. You did it. Yes. Goooood puppy." All that really matters is that the puppy knows you are happy and you issue the praise as soon as the good behavior is completed. Remember: *completed* is the key word. If you are teaching the puppy to come, provide the praise as soon as the puppy arrives (sometimes it even helps to get excited while the puppy is on her way to you). But, if you are teaching the puppy to sit still for a long period of time, then it only stands to reason that you should withhold the praise until the puppy has sat as long as you wanted him to. If the puppy gets up and moves before you give the command, it doesn't make any sense to praise the animal. You need to apply the praise at the right time and withholding praise can often be as effective a training tool as applying it.

Commands

I'll close this discussion with a brief primer on commands. I saved it for the end of the section, so it will be fresh in your mind as you start training your puppy. Commands are the verbal link between you and your puppy. All the other non-verbal dominance behaviors, the use of the leash, and praise and corrections are secondary to the commands you give your puppy. Commands are important enough to puppy training that the two chapters

This puppy is focused on the trainer and waiting for the next command.

Fetch is every puppy's favorite game. Play it often.

that follow will focus on using them effectively. Right now I want to quickly review the commands I suggest you use to train your puppy. You may choose to use others, but if you do, please follow these guidelines. Commands should be:

- One syllable
- Given in a direct and clear voice
- Words that are not easily confused

Here are the basic ones we'll be using. I'll include a short explanation of what *not* to do when you give these commands because, as simple as they seem, if you don't give commands correctly, your training will be all the more difficult.

Sit: This is it. One word. Short and to the point. Don't muck it up by adding anything else, especially the word "down."

Come: This is the command everyone messes up. Don't say things like "C'mere," "here boy," "get here," "over here" or anything else. Just say, "Come."

Heel: When you want the puppy to walk at your side, give this command. Properly teaching a puppy to heel does a lot of things. Most importantly, it teaches the puppy to pay attention to you. When you move, the puppy is to move. When you stop, the puppy is to stop.

"Speak" to the puppy on its own terms, in a language it can understand, and you will be heard.

Down: This is what you say when you want the puppy on its belly. If you forget these commands and later tell your puppy, "Sit Down" the animal will be confused and may not know how to respond.

Fetch: Because this is every puppy's favorite game, you'll want to work this into your training and playtime routines.

A final word on commands: Every dog trainer uses a "release" command, to let the dog know the task is complete and the dog can relax and play. It's kind of like a sergeant telling the troops, "At ease." I typically use the word "okay." Given in a playful tone and followed by a quick "good dog" such a command lets the dog know that immediate task has been finished. Pick a release command and use it when you want the puppy to know he's done and can move on.

As I said at the start, training puppies is not difficult and it doesn't really take a lot of time. What it does take is consistency, repetition and a lot of patience. Puppies are new to your home and will explore the boundaries. They don't do this as an act of defiance; they are just acting out their nature. The older the puppy is when you start the training, the more the puppy will test those boundaries. The animal is just being a puppy, and trying to find its place in your pack. "Speak" to the puppy on its own terms, in a language it can understand, and you will be heard. The best part is, success is easy to see. During each 15-minute segment, you'll begin to realize you are issuing fewer and fewer corrections. You know the training is going well when both you and the puppy are happy during and after the training session.

Where to make it all happen?

Training does not require a huge amount of space or tons of fancy equipment. In fact, I once met a rancher in South Dakota who trained a young cattle dog to respond to its first whistle command while the two rode across the state in the man's pick-up truck. The man wanted the puppy to lie down in response to one short blast of the whistle. After seven hours in the truck, the puppy knew how.

This is an extreme example, but it does present a lot of good information. The training area, in this case the front seat of a pick-up truck, was confined, which meant the puppy couldn't get away. There were also very few distractions, meaning the puppy had to focus on the trainer. Like I said, this training in a truck is an extreme example, but it does provide the combination you want, especially for early training. Once the puppy is responding adequately to your commands in a controlled setting, you can add a few distractions, but start your training where you have complete control and your puppy's undivided attention.

Most puppy owners will do really well working with the puppy in a backyard. It doesn't really need to be fenced because you'll be doing all your early training with the aid of a leash, but if it is, that's all the better.

Lacking a backyard, puppy owners might need to be a bit more creative. Apartment dwellers can work with small puppies right in the hallway, though you may want to go easy on the whistle commands. If there is a

Backyards are great places for training. You have control of everything and the puppy is not distracted.

quiet corner available at a city park, by all means put it to good use. Vacant lots, school playgrounds (when not in use), parking lots (when not busy) and community green spaces all work well as training locations as along as the distractions are few. The idea is that you find a place where the puppy can feel comfortable and concentrate on the training without the sights and sounds of everyday life distracting the young dog from the commands you are giving.

That schedule thing again

Puppies, like all dogs, are creatures of habit. When it comes right down to it, you will be simply just teaching the puppy to get into the habit of obeying you. This will happen much more quickly is the puppy isn't surprised by something new and different each time you snap on the leash. There will be a time when it's important to change the location and the look of the training, but initially, you'll want to go to the same place at the same time. This routine will also help you to stick to your training schedule. The puppy will quickly become comfortable and confident at your training location. This allows the animal to focus on your commands and instructions, thus helping to instill the correct response to those commands. Once your puppy responds to every command while in the controlled setting, it's time to move on to someplace with a few more distractions. Remember everything is a stepping-stone. You are building on each previous success, 15 minutes at time, in order to move up the training ladder.

One benefit of sticking to a training schedule is that the schedule will also help with housebreaking your puppy. Scheduling is one of the key elements in training when and where to do "his business." This is yet another situation that proves the elements of training build on each other by being so entwined that you should not be surprised to find yourself teaching several important things at once. The puppy won't know the difference. Nor will it care. All that the little guy knows is that being with you is fun and if he responds correctly to your commands, it becomes even more fun.

Each training session should be used to teach new skills while you reinforce those things you've already worked on. Always keep in mind that each outing serves to build on the training that came before it. That is how we get the repetition that works so well to train puppies. Be consistent with your commands and every walk to the curb, every trip to the park and every picnic at the lake becomes an additional training experience for the puppy. Follow a schedule, and before long your puppy will be on autopilot.

Give puppies plenty of rest during hot weather fun. When they appear tired, give them a break.

Chapter Six

Puppy Training on Command

To train any dog, you have to use commands. Put simply, commands are how we humans communicate with our dogs. Throughout this chapter I'll talk about issuing commands. You need to understand that you are giving orders. You are not asking, begging or pleading. Tell the pup what to do and require that the puppy obey your command. This is not a request.

When taught properly, the sit command works wonders for keeping a dog under control.

Non-verbal clues, body language and voice inflection all play a huge part in how we communicate with other people, and these are especially important when dealing with puppies. Most communication between canines, especially between a mother dog and a pup, is silent. When she wants to go eat, she steps over the puppies and goes to eat. If a puppy is in the way, she uses her nose to push him out of the way, or she picks him up and carries him.

Your posture can have a huge effect on a young puppy. You are so big, and the puppy is so small, that your demeanor is enough to influence the pup. If you are not careful you can scare the crap out of him, literally, and it could take months to rebuild the dog's trust. So, be calm, but also be direct.

A word about commands: Once

Here's the deal with commands. When dealing with puppies, the commands should be direct, consistent and given clearly either by voice or by whistle. They should also be given once—and only once—and they should be obeyed. The same is true of adult dogs. Luckily, puppies seem to learn faster than adult dogs. Puppies are just waiting for direction. That's why we can get done everything we need to do in a 15-minute training session. These short sessions are easy on us and on the puppies.

From your earliest training sessions you should give your command once, then make sure the puppy understands it and follows the directions. This, of course, is easier said than done. That's because it's human nature to repeat ourselves if we feel we are not heard. It's also true that when we start repeating ourselves we also tend to increase the volume, hoping that what we have to say will eventually inspire the correct actions. This is the wrong thing to do with a puppy because it quickly brings us to the point of yelling and losing our temper, and these are two things that will quickly ruin your training.

If you start down this road of repetition without enforcement, followed by yelling and eventually a complete meltdown, all you are teaching the animal is that it doesn't have to respond on the first command, but it does have to fear you. A puppy's response to a fearful situation is to: 1) cower; 2) attempt to escape; and 3) wet himself. Notice that nowhere do I mention the scared puppy is doing what it is told. It will not. It will cringe. Scream enough times and you'll get the dog to cringe every time it sees you approach. You can, in one 15-minute session, end up with a puppy that is forever afraid of you. That's not the proper use of your 15 minutes.

On the other side of the coin, if the puppy, especially as it approaches 8 or 9 months of age, has even the slightest bit of a defiant streak in its personality you can bet that defiance will appear if you start to repeat your commands. Repeated commands teach a puppy that it has only to respond at some time in the future, if it wants to respond at all. By repeating your commands

When the puppy will sit for extended periods without reminders, you can go on to the next level of training.

Guide the puppy into position. You first must show the puppy what you want. Then you can repeat the sequence and begin training.

you are not advancing to the next level of dominance the way an alpha dog would in a wild pack. You need to up the stakes and do it right away. The two keys to nipping this situation in the bud are control and consistency.

Start with control. All early training must be done on the lead or a long check cord. This gives you total control and the ability to provide instant corrective action if your first command is greeted with a less than enthusiastic response. For instance, if the command "Sit" is given and the puppy does not immediately respond, you can pull up on the short lead, push down on the animal's butt and force compliance. This makes you the dominant one. Without the lead, you are just hoping the puppy will do the right thing. As a rule, use the lead until your puppy complies perfectly every time you issue the command, and then use it for another three to four weeks.

Consistency is also important. If you demand "first-time, every-time" compliance in the yard during training, but resort to giving multiple commands elsewhere, your puppy will quickly know what's happening and will take advantage of the newfound freedom in precisely the place you want total control. With puppies, the place to go off the leash is in the training yard, not out in the park. When the puppy gets it right a dozen times in the yard, then you can try it out in public.

Dog training isn't difficult, but it does take some thought. If we slow down and think about what we are really doing and saying, we can create dogs that respond the first time, every time. This is done by quickly and clearly establishing your dominance.

And remember, we're not getting to that point in our training; we are requiring it right from the start.

Sit: The rock upon which you build your training

Teaching your puppy to sit is the foundation upon which you will build total control. This is where everything starts. The other basic obedience commands, even "heel," will be taught, and very often given, when the puppy is sitting. "Sit" should be thought of as your most powerful command and you should teach it in such a manner that your puppy responds instantly, no matter the circumstances, when you command "Sit." This command is so important you must not only teach it thoroughly, but also reinforce it throughout the rest of your training sessions. If you devote 15 minutes per day to teaching "Sit," any average puppy will master the command inside two weeks. Add two more weeks at 15 minutes each day and you can likely move off the leash for some short sessions.

When you have a dog that sits on command, regardless of the distractions going on all around, you won't have a lot of other problems, especially those associated with a hyperactive puppy. There will be no jumping up, no racing around the yard or the park, no pushing out of the kennel door or bolting into the street. When the dog has been taught to sit, simply give the command, either by voice or with your whistle, and the dog stops whatever he is doing and sits. If you teach your puppy nothing else in the world you should be set on mastering this one simple command. It will give you control of your dog.

Right now you're likely saying, "Sure, that sounds great. But this is a 3-month-old puppy. How do I do it?" If you want your puppy to drop its butt to the ground every time you issue the command, let's start by reviewing your part.

- The voice command is "Sit" and the corresponding whistle command is a single, short blast on the whistle.
- Training must begin on the leash, especially for older puppies. Keep the pup on the leash until you are confident that you have control.
- Give the command once, then reinforce it by showing the puppy exactly what you expect. Do not repeat the command.

If we slow down and think about what we are really doing and saying, we can create dogs that respond the first time, every time.

Make sure the collar is attached firmly to the leash.

As I mentioned above, start training with the leash securely clipped to the puppy's collar. Now start walking. This will get the puppy on its feet and provide an initial distraction that the puppy must overcome. After a few steps stop, give one blast on your whistle and say, "Sit." Then, while holding the leash tightly, gently but firmly push down on the puppy's butt, directing the animal to the sitting position. As soon as the puppy's hindquarters hit the ground, pet him on the head and offer lots of praise.

This type of training actually teaches two things at once. By using the leash and taking a few steps before giving the command, the puppy is also learning to sit at your side each time you stop walking, which is very nice when you are out for a stroll. But let's get back to the original lesson.

You've commanded, "Sit" and guided the puppy to the sitting position. Now you praise him. With most puppies, this praise will be enough to make the dog break from the sitting position. That's fine. Don't get upset. This is all part of the training. As soon as the puppy breaks, give a short tug on the leash (this is your correction) and, if you need to, push down on the dog's butt to return the animal to the sitting position. Now, stand still and count silently to five or 10 before praising the puppy. If the puppy moves before you are done counting do not repeat the command, but do repeat the correction. By doing this you are teaching the puppy to sit until you say it's time to move again.

After you've counted to five or 10, praise the puppy lavishly and repeat the process. Your goal is to slowly increase the amount of time you require your puppy to sit in one place before you offer praise. During the first day of training, you might issue the command a dozen times, each time counting to 10. The next day, go through the same sequence but count to 20. In most cases, you'll be able to quit pushing down on the puppy's butt after about the third day. By that time, the puppy understands what "Sit" means and is now just waiting for the praise and your permission to once again move about.

Tell your puppy to "Sit," then gently, but firmly, show it exactly what you want it to do.

At this point, both you and your pet are learning about patience. It is difficult to imagine anything more boring than standing beside a dog that's trained well enough to sit still for several minutes. But you have to do it to keep the dog from moving until you say it's time to move. I think the longest I've gone, using my wristwatch as a timer, is five minutes. It seems like an eternity, but I figure that if the dog will sit still for five full minutes, it's time to move on to the next phase of training.

The "surprise" command

I can't stress enough that teaching your puppy to sit on command will be the foundation on which everything else is built. Practice daily until it is mastered (you'll be surprised how quickly a dog will catch on), but also include some playtime. At the end of each session, wrestle around on the ground with the puppy or toss a retrieval dummy or a Frisbee a few feet away and let the puppy get used to picking it up. The puppy needs this kind of fun and affection after a training session—it helps build the bond between you and the puppy. It also gives you the opportunity to sneak in some very important training while you play.

It's called training with (or through) distractions. After you've finished the bread and butter of your "real" training session and you've decided to spend a little bit of playtime with the puppy, go ahead and get rough. Keep the puppy on the leash, but play around. Chase the puppy. Let him chase you. Wrestle a bit. Roll toys around. Do whatever it is you and your puppy do for fun. Then, just as the puppy's really getting into it, really having a great time, spring a good firm "Sit" command on her.

To encourage compliance with this sort of surprise or "snap" command, make sure that you stop moving around as soon as you issue the command. It's not really fair to expect a puppy in the early stages of training to sit still while you're still running around playing games. That's just too much distraction at this stage of the training. The goal of this type of snap command is to remind the puppy that "Sit" (like all the other basic commands) is an absolute command that must be obeyed without hesitation each time it is given. By giving the command during playtime, you are reinforcing on the puppy the idea that you set the schedule, you make the decisions and you give the orders. This is done with the leash still attached to the puppy's collar so you can get control quickly if you need to and administer a correction if the puppy fails to respond.

Even a "snap" command should get an immediate response.

When you can command your dog to sit, even if the animal is a block away, you have complete control of the dog and people will think you are a miracle worker.

The sequence for praising the puppy following a snap command is just the same as before. At first you can praise right away if you want to, but by this time, your puppy will likely understand that "Sit" means she is not to move until you say so. If that's the case and you can spring a snap "Sit" command and your puppy remains rock steady for five minutes or more. You can go on to additional training.

The next phase is being able to give the command from a distance. This is the really cool stuff! When you can command your dog to sit, even if the animal is a block away, you can be assured of two things: you have complete control of the dog and people who know you will think you are a miracle worker. The best part is that it's so simple anyone can do it.

After your puppy sits for as long as you can put up with standing by its side, try backing away. Initially, you won't be backing away too far. The first step here is to move from the side of the puppy to directly in front of it. At this time you'll still be holding the leash.

The average puppy will think that you are starting to walk again and move to go with you. Give a bit of a correction and hold your hand, palm facing the puppy, directly in front of the puppy's nose. You are teaching the dog that the "Sit" command must be obeyed, even if the master moves. So, start by giving the command. Once the puppy is sitting, step in front of her. Correct and reinforce with the leash and your hand as needed. When the

Now that you have your puppy's attention, issue your next command.

puppy remains still for a 10-count, take a step backwards. Count again and take another step backwards.

If you haven't figured it out by now, you'll quickly notice that you are putting enough distance between you and the puppy so as to make your typical correction with the leash difficult or even impossible.

A correction at any distance is a bit more difficult, which I why I stress close control for the early stages of this training. At close range you can administer a correction almost instantly and with very little effort. Once the puppy sits, and knows to sit until you say otherwise, there is much less chance that you'll have to correct from a distance. But let's say your star pupil has learned to sit so well you practically fall asleep waiting for the animal to break. Now it's clearly time to start giving the command at a distance. You issue the command, step in front of the puppy and back up three full steps. At this time, the puppy breaks and starts leaning forward as if to take a step forward. What do you do?

Hold out your hand, palm facing the puppy, and say, "No," in a firm voice. This should stop the advance. Count to five, then walk to the puppy and praise him for listening so well.

If, on the other hand, the puppy does not stop when you say, "No," don't wait for her to come to you. Walk toward her calmly, pick her up and place her gently back where she was sitting. Then give the sit command again and back away only two steps and make her sit for a count of 20 before you praise her.

The idea is to each day increase the distance and the time a little bit more. You want the puppy to understand that even if you are far away, "Sit" means just that.

As this training continues your leash will become too short. Your long training cord may become too short, too. Don't worry. Leave either attached to the puppy and drop it on the ground. If the puppy breaks, hold up your hand, command, "No," walk over, pick up the puppy and drop him on his original spot. Then start the training again. If, when you let go of the leash or the training cord, the puppy runs off, you have a really good indication that you've got to go back a few steps in the training, but you'll also have a longer "handle" on which to grab if you need to chase down the wayward hound.

At this point, some of you might be asking, "What happened to 'Stay'—aren't you forgetting something?" Frankly, I've never understood why some people tell dogs to "Stay." If you teach "Sit" effectively, you shouldn't have to take the time to teach the dog another command to keep it in place. "Sit"

Frankly, I've never understood why some people tell dogs to "Stay." If you teach "Sit" effectively, you shouldn't have to teach the dog another command to keep it in place.

The leash is an essential tool for convincing puppies that commands must be obeyed—even when given from a distance.

means sit until a release command is given. Of course the dog will stay.

Let's get back to this sitting-at-a-distance business. Once you've successfully backed all the way to the end of your long training cord, you've really done nothing more than teach the puppy to *stay sitting* while you are not nearby. But that's a good start and another important building block in the training foundation. To teach the puppy to *sit at a distance*, you have to get the animal moving a bit. So, back up to the end of the long training cord and give it a little tug and call the puppy's name and say, "Come." (We're not actually teaching the puppy to come just yet; this is just a by-product of the sit command. It also shows how everything about training a puppy is so intertwined.) As the puppy moves forward, take up the slack a bit to make sure the puppy is moving directly toward you. When the animal gets about halfway to you give a blast on the whistle if you are using one and, say, "Sit" as you hold your hand with your palm facing the puppy.

One of these three indicators should prompt the puppy to sit right where you told her to. If they do not, approach the puppy (calmly, don't charge at her), pick her up and set her gently down where you asked her to sit. Then back up to the end of the training cord and try again. Puppies will figure this out in a hurry, but as the handler you still need to be patient, calm and persistent.

As the puppy learns to sit still no matter what you do or where you are, you can introduce more and more temptations and distractions. My favorite test is to tell the puppy to "Sit," and then go hide. Once I'm out of the puppy's line of sight, I try to move to a position where I can see the puppy, but she can't see me. Then I'll wait and see what the animal does. If I've succeeded in thoroughly teaching the puppy to sit, the animal will look around for a little while and eventually just lie down and wait for me to return. That's when I know the training is progressing as it should.

Advanced "Sit" training (to be covered in a later chapter) includes huge distractions, up to and including requiring the puppy to sit still even as other dogs romp around and play with their masters. When your puppy will sit through such an outing, you've achieved something spectacular.

Come: The command no one wants to repeat

So, now that your puppy will stay sitting while you wash and wax the car, what's next?

Having a puppy that will come when it's called is always nice. It's more than nice—it is a requirement. If you don't mind chasing your puppy all over town, or sitting on the front porch waiting for him to return; if you want to be able control your pup at a distance to keep her away from dangerous situations; if you want to prove to the neighbors that they have nothing to fear when you let your puppy go for a run, then your puppy needs to come when called. And again, the puppy should respond the first time you call and come every time. There can be nothing more important to your puppy than responding to your command to "Come."

That, of course leads us to the same old question, "How do we get there?" Once again I'll tell you that we don't get there, we start there.

Back when I was trying to train my very first dog, I watched a video that showed a dog sitting in a field and running to its master's side after a single blast on the whistle. The announcer went on to say, "This seemingly simple task requires the training of no less than 12 different commands and takes months to master." My first thought was, "It can't be that hard." I was right. It's not really that hard at all.

While there may be tons of subtle nuances you can introduce and describe as training steps for calling a dog, when it comes right down to it, teaching a puppy to come is just about the easiest thing in the world once you've trained the animal to sit. Get yourself about 25 feet of rope and attach a snap loop on the end. Hook it to the dog's collar. Command the dog to "Sit," and then back away about 10 feet. Kneel down. Give several quick blasts on the whistle, say the puppy's name, and then say, "Come." That should start the animal moving in your direction. If she turns or stops, pull on the rope just like you are reeling in a fish and say, "Come." When the puppy arrives, lavish the animal with praise. Then, command "Sit," back up a bit farther and try it again.

This puppy is waiting to be called. But is the toy too much of a distraction?

You'll notice that I use a whistle right from the beginning when teaching a dog to come. You'll find out early on that whistles carry much better than your voice. A whistle can be heard above the din of road noise, over the voices of children playing in the parks and across all but the biggest ponds. With the exception of blowing a whistle during a stiff headwind, you can believe that your puppy has heard the whistle command. If the dog doesn't come when you blow the thing, he may be ignoring you, which means you've got some more training to do with the long cord.

So, let's go back to a discussion of the early training for "Come." You want to make yourself as inviting as possible when teaching the puppy to come. The goal is to make the puppy happy to see you and happy to be by your side. I've heard all sorts of advice on using treats as a reward for a proper response. Some trainers say it's the only way to teach a dog to come; others have told me, "When you're out of treats, you're out of luck." Well, then, maybe just plan ahead and don't run out of treats. The flipside of that discussion is that praise should usually be effective enough as a reward to get a puppy to come to you. If you are down there at puppy level, talking in a happy voice, 99 percent of all puppies will come to you, especially if you are pulling on the rope to provide a little bit of guidance. I come down on the side of avoiding treats mostly because they teach dog owners to get away with poor training habits. Good training and lots of praise will work every time.

While there are lots of things you can do to get a puppy to come to you, there also some things you shouldn't do.

Never call the dog in an angry voice. Never, never, NEVER hit the animal when it arrives. To do so is punishing the puppy for doing what you asked. Any dog that's even halfway smart will think twice about coming to you when you call if the result is a beating. This bears repeating and I don't think I can stress it enough. Puppies know when you are angry. In most cases tone of voice is the only thing you need to use to let the pup know how you feel. Yet, no matter how far off the puppy runs, what it has done while it was away or how frustrated you are by the animal's continued desire to romp

Yes it was. In this case a leash or check cord could enforce the command.

After telling the puppy to "Come," a steady tug reinforces the command.

It doesn't take long for the puppy to figure out what's expected of him.

about without listening to a word you are saying, NEVER punish a dog for coming to you. To do so is not only cruel, but will also totally disrupt any training you are trying to accomplish.

Also, pay close attention to the command you are giving. The command is, "Come." It is not, "Come 'ere. Here boy. Get here. Come on" or anything else you might decide to say. For consistency's sake, the command should also be preceded by several short blasts on the whistle. This is especially important early in the training, when you are encouraging the dog to respond to both your voice and the whistle. As the training progresses, you can call just by voice or just with the whistle. Indeed, you should mix in a couple of each of these commands during each training session just to let your puppy know that, regardless of which command (voice or whistle), she should respond immediately.

Lavish praise—no matter how much he resisted—is the best reward. Never get angry, or the puppy will think that "Come" means punishment.

Now, if you're starting with a dog you've rescued from the local animal shelter, your on-leash training will run a little longer than the training an 8-week-old pup will require. Don't get frustrated. As before, this is just a matter of teaching the puppy new rules. You use the rope to reinforce the fact that when you call, the puppy can do nothing other than come to you. This is not a game. It is not playtime. This is serious business and there can only be one proper response when you call. It's important that you create a happy atmosphere surrounding the issuance of the command. But let there be no confusion between either you or the dog, it still is a command. You issue it. The dog obeys it. No discussion.

Those last three little sentences work very well for younger dogs, but, as always, those "problem cases" require more patience and several weeks of repetitive training on the leash before you can even think about releasing the line and hoping the dog will come when you call. If you are working with an older pup or a young dog rescued from the shelter, you should consider the animal untrained or under-trained. These dogs have a wonderful memory for what it's like to be free from the confines of things like commands and leashes. I once worked daily for six weeks with an untrained 3-year-old German shorthair pointer. The dog was kept on the leash the entire time. At the end of 42 days the dog responded like a show champion to every command I gave. On day 43 I decided to remove the leash. Almost before the snap hit the ground that dog had shifted into high gear. Three hours later a muddy, tired-looking pointer showed up at my front door and I snapped on the leash and continued the on-leash work for another four weeks.

A good rule of thumb is to train on the leash until you think the dog has the command mastered, then train for two more weeks before opening the snap. Even then, keep off-leash training sessions short and keep the dog close by until you are sure every command you give will be followed.

A good rule of thumb is to train on the leash until you think the dog has the command mastered, then train for two more weeks before opening the snap.

Some puppies just seem to figure out the difference between being on the leash and being free of it. When you find a dog that smart, you have to be very careful about how you conduct your off-leash training. Often it becomes a matter of starting almost at the beginning of your training cycle, except now you've removed the leash. That's to say, after the puppy responds perfectly—even from extended distances—on the leash, you have to start over by keeping the animal very close to you as you first let go of the leash.

You read that correctly. Don't unhook the leash. Just let go of it. That way you have what amounts to an extended "handle" if the puppy tries to get away. And, if you plant your foot firmly on the leash your pup is dragging away, he administers his own instant correction.

Combining lessons

Just because you are now teaching the dog to come, does not mean that you should abandon work on the "Sit" command. On the contrary, now is the perfect time to combine some of the lessons to really reinforce the building-block philosophy of training.

After your puppy is coming to you while on the long leash (which may even be the first day of training), it's time to spring a surprise command just to make sure the dog is paying attention. Give the command, "Sit" and back away. After a few seconds, call the puppy to "Come." When the animal is halfway to you, step forward, hold out one hand and say, "Sit." The puppy will, at first, be a bit confused. After all, you just called and now you are changing your mind. The best part is, it's your right. You can change your mind any time you want and puppy must listen.

Anyway, chances are your puppy will not stop right away the first time you try this. If the dog keeps coming after you command, "Sit," take a few more steps forward and give the puppy a good stern look in the eye. You might want to add the word "No" at this time, but the object is to do as little talking as possible. If the pup stops, but does not sit, approach it and push down on its butt, while pulling up on the leash. When the dog is sitting, provide lots of praise while you rub on the shoulders. Then command, "Sit" and back away again to start the process over.

Some professional trainers to use a gadget called a "whoa pole" for this type of training. It's really nothing more than a post in the ground with a ring attached firmly to it. The long leash (in this case a really long line) is run through the loop and attached to the collar. The puppy is commanded to sit and the handler backs away, holding the bitter end of the line. When

Puppies are all about fun. Have some fun with yours.

the puppy is called the trainer lets the line flow until it is time to command, "Sit." The command is issued, and trainer grabs the line and hangs on, jerking the puppy to a stop. Gloves are advised.

This type of training goes a bit beyond basic, but it is sometimes required for really stubborn dogs.

It's important to mix up the sequence, sometimes letting the puppy come all the way to you while at other times ordering her to stop. The goal is to remind her that you are in control and the last command is always the one to listen to, even if it is the direct opposite of one given before it. So, mix things up a little bit. As we continue to add more commands to the training sessions, the opportunities to build on the lessons of the past increase. This keeps things interesting for both you and the dog and insures that past training is not forgotten even as new lessons are incorporated.

So, remember the goal. You want the dog to come the first time you call. To achieve this, use the long line well after you think you don't need it anymore. Training like this, 15 minutes at a time, three to five times a week, will really put you on the road to creating a great puppy.

Chapter Seven

Commands, Part 2: Heel and Down

Who wants to walk the dog? If that question gets nothing but groans of displeasure around your house, this chapter is for you. Every dog needs to have good manners, both on the leash and off, but teaching a dog to properly heel will make your life as a dog owner infinitely less frustrating and will very likely improve your attitude about walking the dog. And that says nothing about how much more fun the dog will have during your walks.

A dog that won't heel can be a pain when it comes time for a walk. Good training will overcome this.

Before we really get into teaching the puppy to heel, a short discussion about the leash is in order. Up to this point, the leash served only as a restraint—the word I like to use is "handle." It's something you grab onto to hold the dog, guide the dog to the sitting position or pull the puppy to you when teaching him to come. When you are teaching the puppy to heel, there are some subtleties about the leash you should consider. First and foremost is to match the size of the leash to the size of the dog. You don't need 10 feet of half-inch rope to control a 10-week-old pup.

For general training to heel and for most walks, a 6-foot leash is just fine if you match the weight of the material to the size of the dog. Get a good commercially made leash. You can make up your own long check cord for other training, but for your everyday leash purchase something good. Make sure the snap is stout, but easy to use, and always think about how the material feels in your hand.

Now we are ready to go. Through your work with the earlier commands, your puppy should understand by now what the leash is and how it will be used. The key to this exercise is to get the dog to concentrate on you and react to your movements when you issue the command.

Teaching these lessons is the same for all dogs. We start again with the leash clipped to the collar. Give the command "Sit" and stand beside the dog for a few seconds. If the dog still hasn't mastered sitting, stand for up to a

Always conduct your training sessions with the puppy on a leash. Get a good collar that fits and a leash that doesn't overwhelm the small dog.

minute. Then, without warning, start walking. As soon as you move your first foot, say, "Heel" and give a gentle tug to get the dog going. Now that you're both moving, pay attention to the puppy. What you are after is a puppy that walks between 12 inches and 36 inches from your side and just about even with you. I've always allowed my dogs to be about a pace ahead when I say "Heel," just so I can see the animal. You decide what you're comfortable with and be consistent. Don't allow the puppy to run to the end of the leash one day, and then require the animal brush up against your knee the next. You'll confuse the critter.

When teaching your dog to heel, be consistent. For the record, almost all dog professional trainers put their dogs on the left. That's because when all dogs were used for hunting the trainers carried a shotgun in their right hand. So, for the sake of consistency and tradition, keep the dog on your left side.

If the dog rushes ahead to the end of the leash, gather up about a foot of slack and give the leash a sharp jerk, while simultaneously issuing the "Heel" command quite firmly. Don't shout, but be firm. Remember, this is a puppy, not a 60-pound Husky. It doesn't take much to be firm with a puppy.

At this stage in the training, take about 10 steps forward then turn away from the puppy; give a moderate tug on the leash and say, "Heel." The idea is to make the dog pay attention to what you are doing. At first you'll be pretty

A small tug is all that is needed to correct a pup.

much walking in a big square, but you can do some things to add a bit of variety. Change your pace. Walk quickly. Jog if you like. Then, creep along slowly as if you are sneaking up on something. All the while, keep a firm grip on the leash and make corrections, if needed, as described above.

After a few sessions of always turning the same way, change directions. You will find your dog expecting you to turn the other way and your knee will bump the puppy's shoulder as you turn into him. No problem, just nudge the pup out of the way like you know where you're going. Soon, the puppy will begin to pay very close attention to you and react instantly as you start walking, change directions or stop. This is exactly what you want. When you command the puppy to heel, she should be focused totally on what you are doing. She should be your little canine shadow. One of the best ways to encourage this is to make frequent turns as you are walking the dog. By doing so, you'll either bump the dog or tug on the leash and either way; you'll be focusing the animal's attention on your actions. Soon, it will become second nature to the puppy to focus only on you.

When you stop walking, immediately command the puppy to "Sit." This will teach her that her place is by your side. Reinforce this and your puppy will understand that she must stay put until to you say it's fine to leave. The reinforcement also triples your dog's training while requiring no extra training time. During a single 15-minute lesson of teaching the puppy to heel, you'll also be reinforcing the "Sit" command and teaching the dog to sit every time you stop. This is where the training really starts to multiply. The puppy

Don't unhook the leash too soon. Puppies learn quickly, but that also means they learn quickly to see when they are not on the leash.

is learning lots of things and you are teaching more than you ever thought you could in such a short period. Best of all, neither of you really notice how much is being done.

Use caution

A word of warning here about starting to work the puppy without the leash: You've read it before—don't unhook the leash too soon. Puppies learn quickly, but that also means they learn quickly to see when they are not on the leash. For you to consistently repeat your training sequence you must have control of the puppy through a leash. Once the dog follows each of the basic commands flawlessly while on the leash, keep the thing on for another week or two—and then think about unclipping the animal for advanced work.

Oh yeah, the advanced work!

As simple as it is to get a dog to heel, it is also equally simple to let the dog slip back into bad habits. That, in turn, draws you into bad habits. You see, as the puppy creeps farther and farther away after you've commanded the animal to heel, you end up issuing the command again and again. Thus, you are teaching the puppy to ignore the first command and only listen after you've talked yourself blue in the face.

To keep this from happening, use the leash often. Use the leash when you don't think you'll need it. Use it after you're sure that your puppy has mastered the command. Use it occasionally without rhyme or reason and always issue corrections without words. A short sharp tug will say more than you ever can.

Working off the leash comes only after the command is mastered and the dog is listening.

Once you have the puppy accustomed to the idea that once you command "Heel," he should go everywhere you go, it's time to work without the leash. After a week or so most puppies start to really understand what "Heel" means. It's then that you can drop the leash on the ground, letting the puppy drag it alongside you. If the dog starts to move too far ahead of you or off to one side, just step down on the leash. Boink! Instant correction, and the dog did all the work.

Working with the leash dragging is also a good way to teach the dog to get into position when you command, "Heel." I require that my dogs stand beneath my left hand when I'm stopped and I command, "Heel." When walking, they can move a bit in front of me, but still on the left. So no matter what I'm doing or what the dog is doing, when I call, then command the dog to "Heel," I want the animal on my left. To teach that is a simple matter of encouraging the puppy to move into that position by turning away from the animal and patting your hand against your left leg when you say, "Heel."

Here's how it's done. Command the dog to "Sit" and back away. Command the dog to "Come." When the animal gets more than half way to you, command, "Heel," turn your back to the dog and pat your left leg, so the puppy comes to that spot. Then, just as the dog gets there, turn around again and pat your left leg, so the dog follows the patting sound around behind you. When you stop moving, the puppy should sit at your side. Then lavish on the praise. Incorporate several of these movements into each training session and pretty soon your dog will automatically fall in at your side when you say, "Heel."

When the training goes right, issue lots of praise for your puppy.

That's really about all there is to teaching a puppy to heel. All of these practices can be applied not just during training sessions, but also during every walk in the park or trip around the block. Consistency is the key to success. If you refuse to let the dog yank at the leash and provide consistent commands and corrections, those daily walks will become a fun activity for you and your puppy.

Down: It's really just an advanced version of sit

When you want your dog to lie down, nothing else will really do. It's important to understand that when you command your dog, "Down," it's really like an extension of the command, "Sit." Both commands do about the same thing in that they require the dog to remain in one place until you command otherwise. But "Down" offers the added benefit of reinforcing your dominance. In short, when you make a dog lie down it's a lot like you are putting your hands on his shoulders. Remember that from a previous

A clear visual indicator helps the puppy learn to lie down. Puppies like to see what they are supposed to do.

> Teach "Down" well and you'll never again find yourself grabbing an overly excited dog by the collar and dragging her off to the porch or the bedroom.

chapter? A dog that is down is agreeing to assume a submissive posture. That alone may be enough to make training this command a bit more difficult with some strong-willed dogs. With older, untrained or under-trained dogs, teaching "Down" can be downright frustrating—but don't give up.

"Down" is a great command for extended rests. If you're sitting in a park reading, watching the kids' Little League game or anywhere you'll be in one spot for a while, give the "Down" command and, if your training has gone well, you can just about forget about the dog for a while. One more reason to teach the command well is that it provides another level of control in several situations, not the least important is when visitors (especially new visitors) drop by your home or apartment. Life is so much easier when you can simply give the dog a one-word command. Teach "Down" well and you'll never again find yourself grabbing an overly excited dog by the collar and dragging her off to the porch or the bedroom as you tell your guest, "Wow, she really likes you."

One reminder: The command is "Down." Forget about all those other things you might be tempted to say. Be simple, be direct and be consistent. Doing so will make the training easier on both you and the dog–not that this operation is all that difficult to accomplish in the first place.

Here's what you'll do. To teach the dog to get on it's belly, you'll need to have control of the animal. As mentioned above, getting a dog to lie down on command is an act of dominance. If a dog wants to lie down on its own, well, that's another story. But when you make a dog lie down, it's a clear sign that you are in charge. To that end, you'll need to start with the dog on the leash.

Clip on the leash and walk slowly around your training area. If you've recently been working on "Heel" your dog will likely sit every time you stop. That's fine. In fact, that's great because a sitting dog is halfway to down. When you stop walking, command, "Sit" and allow the dog to comply. Once the dog is sitting, command, "Down," and immediately step down on the slack part of the leash close to the dog's collar. The downward pressure pushes the animal's forequarters to the turf with very little effort on your part. Issue praise immediately.

Ideally, you want the dog down, but in an erect posture. Think of the Sphinx—that's a beautiful posture for a dog in the down position.

The rest of the training should progress pretty much like teaching the dog to sit. Once you've commanded, "Down" and guided the dog to its belly, you can praise him. If your dog has mastered the "Sit" command, you should have no trouble with the dog breaking—that is, moving—from the down position. Just for the sake of training—or if you've decided to teach "Down"

Working with two puppies can be a challenge. Better to avoid the distractions and do the early training separately.

before you teach "Sit"—let's assume the dog breaks. Just like I said in the chapter on teaching the dog to sit, don't get upset. Breaking is part of the training. It happens; you just train through it.

As soon as the dog breaks, give a short tug on the leash (this is your correction) and, if you need to, push down on the dog's shoulders to return the animal to the down position. Now, stand still and count silently to five or 10 before praising the dog. If the dog moves before you are done counting, do not repeat the command, but do repeat the correction. By doing this you are teaching the dog to stay down until you say it's time to move again.

After you've counted to five or 10, praise the dog lavishly and repeat the process. Your goal is to slowly increase the amount of time you require your dog to lie in one place before you offer praise. During the first day of training, you might issue the command a half-dozen times, each time counting to 10. If you've taught the dog to sit, you may have no trouble at all. The next day, go through the same sequence, but count to 20. In most cases, you'll be able to quit pushing down on the dog's shoulders in very short order—three days, tops. By that time, the dog understands what "Down" means and is waiting for the praise and your permission to once again move around.

I'm repeating myself from the chapter on sitting, but once again both you and your pet are learning about patience. It is difficult to imagine anything more boring than standing beside a dog that's trained well enough to lie still for several minutes. But you have to do it. Five minutes may seem like an eternity, but I figure that if a dog will lie still for five full minutes, it's time to move onto the next phase of training.

The "Surprise" command again

Once the dog will go down and remain steady, it's time to include some playtime. Get wild, wrestle around on the ground with the dog or toss a ball or a Frisbee a few feet away and let the dog get used to picking it up. You did this while teaching the dog to sit and it will work just as well with "Down." Now you are going to sneak in some very important training while you play.

Your dog needs to work through distractions. After you've finished the "real" training session and you've decided to spend a little bit of playtime do whatever it is you and your dog do for fun. Then, just as the dog is really getting into it, spring a good firm "Down" command on her.

Again, I'm repeating myself here, but repetition is the key to good training. To encourage compliance with this sort of surprise, or "snap," command, make sure that you stop moving around as soon as you issue the command.

Correct problems by kneeling down and calmly, gently putting the dog into the position you want while repeating the command once.

The goal of this type of snap command is to remind the dog that "Down" (like all the other commands) is an absolute command that must be obeyed without hesitation each time it is given. By giving the command during playtime, you are reinforcing on the dog the idea that you set the schedule, you make the decisions, and you give the orders. This is done with the leash still attached to the dog's collar so you can get control quickly if you need to, and administer a correction if the dog fails to respond.

The sequence for praising the dog following a snap command is just the same as before. At first you can praise right away if you want to, but by this time your dog will likely understand that "Down" means he is not to move until you say so. The dog is simply lying there looking at you, not moving, waiting for the praise to come. A well-trained dog will wait all day for that praise. If that's the case, you can spring a snap command and your dog remains rock steady for five minutes or more. You can go on to additional training.

But wait—before you do that, you'll also want to make minor adjustments to the dog's posture. You don't want the animal rolling over to its side, or, worse yet, on its back. If the dog tends to do this, that's a sure sign the animal is feeling a little too submissive. To correct the problem, you simply correct the problem. Kneel down and physically, but calmly and gently, put the dog into the position you want. At this time you can repeat the command, once. You'll say, "Down" as you do this, just to let the dog know what you expect after the command. The dog has to know what it is you want, before it will remember the training sessions.

Distance learning

The next phase is being able to give the command from a distance. This is the really cool stuff. When you can command your dog to sit, even if the animal is a block away, all your neighbors will look at you with awe and wonder how you've learned to work such magic. The best part is that it's so simple anyone can do it.

After your dog stays down for as long as you can put up with standing by its side, try backing away. Just like in the chapter on "Sit," you initially will not be backing away too far. The first step here is to move from the side of the dog to directly in front of it. Then back up two steps. At this time you'll still be holding the leash.

Call the dog to you, command the animal to "Sit" and offer some praise. Back up to the end of your leash. If your dog learned the "Sit" command this should be no trouble. Now command "Down" and give the dog a few

> By giving a command during playtime, you are reinforcing the idea that you set the schedule, you make the decisions, and you give the orders.

Even a distraction failed to cause this well-mannered pup to break.

seconds to respond. If there is now movement, approach the dog and gently but firmly push down on the shoulders, then back up to the end of the leash. Count to five and offer praise.

A correction at any distance is a bit tough, which is why I stress close control for the early stages of the distance "Down" as well as the "Sit" command. At close range you can administer a correction quickly and get the dog to comply promptly. One trick is to back up the length of your short leash and, as you issue the "Down" command, bend at the knees and point to the ground. This usually gets the dog moving in the right direction. Some might call it cheating, but if it works, I consider it a good option.

Praise for the distance "Down" is another key to getting a decent response. If, at a distance of about 6 feet (the length of your short leash), your dog drops to her belly on command, pause for a moment before you offer the praise. Then, praise lavishly. Give treats if you want to, but by all means let the dog know you are happy. If the dog does not drop immediately, offer no praise. By this point in the training, your dog should be conditioned to the fact that the proper response to a command earns praise. If the dog fails to respond as ordered, there is no happy talk, no treats, nothing. All that should happen is that you walk up and put the dog in the down position.

As with teaching "Sit" from a distance, the idea here is to each day increase the distance from which you give the command, and the time the dog is required to remain down. You want the dog to understand that even if you are far away, "Down," means just that.

As this training continues, your leash will become too short. Your long check cord may become too short, too. Don't worry. For this type of training, the cord is not really used for much of anything other than a reminder that you are in control. You can't use the check cord, or even a leash for that matter, to force a dog down from a distance. You have to walk over and force the issue from close range.

This is usually the time that dog owners find out how much their dogs really love them. It happens like this: The dog is down at a distance and has actually dropped quickly to the command, leading you to believe everything is great. But, before too long, the dog starts to creep forward in an effort to be closer to you. It's actually rather comical to see a dog trying to low-crawl "unnoticed" in the direction of his best buddy. As funny as it looks, you should nip this in the bud right away.

Faced with a creeping dog, the average person will probably want to say, "Stay" to stop this behavior. Let me remind you again about the command—actually the pseudo-command—"Stay." If you teach "Down" effectively, you shouldn't have to take the time to teach the dog another command to keep it in place. As with "Sit," "Down" means no movement is allowed until a release command is given. Of course the dog will stay. Don't waste your breath and confuse the dog with a command that is not required.

The best thing you can do when a dog is trying to creep from the down position is to provide a good, firm, "No." Combine that with a menacing stare and some more of the good power-posture stuff and your dog will stop creeping in short order.

"Down" is a great command and a great place to be in your training. A dog that has mastered all the basic commands is a pleasure to be around. Once you get to this point, you have very few worries and your frustration factor, as it relates to how your dog responds to commands, should be very low.

Sit. Come. Heel. Down. You've got what a professional dog trainer would call a "started dog" and what most Americans would call a great pet.

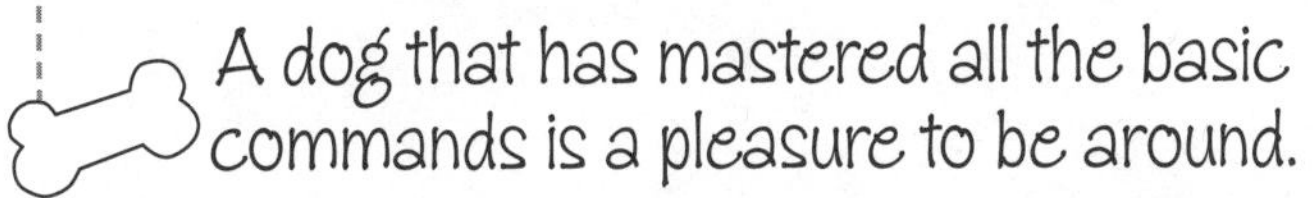

Chapter Eight

Beyond the Basics

If your puppy comes when you call, stands at your side when you command "Heel" and sits on command, you can start working on the fancy stuff: retrieving. In reality, you can start working on retrieves even before your puppy has mastered the other commands, but it will be more difficult. My advice is to get the basics down first. Then move on.

All dogs will retrieve. In fact, when looking for potential drug-sniffing dogs, law enforcement agencies don't usually check pedigrees. They just want a dog that will willingly and excitedly retrieve all day long. With that attitude, they can sculpt a canine cop.

Fetch: Pup's favorite game

You can teach any puppy to fetch without much trouble at all, if you just continue building on the foundations we've established. Remember, all we are trying to do is show the dog what we want, then repeat the activity until it becomes second nature. My first rule of retrieving is this: It's only a game. So, I'll say it again: No hitting, shouting or pinching. It's all about making the puppy *want* to bring something back to you. The first part of that is making sure the dog loves the game. The game has to be the greatest thing since doggie treats. Retrieving always has to be fun.

But, I'm getting ahead of myself. Let's start with something really simple. What should your puppy fetch? Well, first off, not sticks. A dog running with a stick in its mouth is an accident waiting for a big vet bill. You would never send your child to get you a long pointed object and tell the kid, "Go get that! Run!" Not that I believe dogs and children are on the same level, but I do believe that you should never do something that you know has the potential to cause serious injury. So, you can use tennis balls, Frisbees, a rolled up towel secured with duct tape, a ball of twine… just about anything that isn't sharp. My personal favorite is the product that is designed for just

Unless you plan on playing tug-of-war every time you send pup to fetch, teach the dog to give the ball on command.

such an activity: the dog-training dummy or bumper. They are available at just about any sporting goods store or through most sporting goods mail-order or Internet retailers. Dummies come in a variety of sizes and colors and will nearly always stand up to the toughest dogs.

So, grab one and get the puppy excited about it. Start playing with the dog, swinging the dummy around the dog's nose, dragging it on the ground, just out of reach. Talk in an excited manner and try to keep the dog interested. If the dog is lucky enough to get hold of the dummy, don't pull it away, just say, "Good dog!" and heap on the praise. Then, gently but firmly remove the dummy from her mouth and start again. While this is going on, drop in a "Sit" command, just to reinforce old habits. You are doing this to remind the dog that even though something fun is happening, obedience must still be observed. If the dog responds properly, and it should by this time, you are ready for your first toss. It will be a short one.

Put the puppy on a long leash at heel and keep the animal by your side with a "Sit" command. Toss the dummy 10 to 15 feet in front of the dog, and hold the leash. Do not let the dog rush off until you say so. After a short wait, maybe five or 10 seconds, give the command "Fetch!" and point to the dummy. As soon as the dog picks up the dummy, call the dog back. If everything goes according to plan, the dog should come right back. If not, you can pull on the rope to reel the dog in.

Now, you have to get the dummy. This is the only place I will get a bit forceful with a dog. For me, a game of tug-of-war is not part of learning to retrieve. But it may be for you. If you want the dog to deliver fetched objects right to your hand and let go on command, tell the dog, "Give" and immediately take the dummy. If the dog does not want to let go, grab the lower jaw and squeeze a bit while you pull down. As soon as the dummy is in your hand, praise the dog lavishly.

During this cycle of training it is especially important to create good habits and be careful not to instill any bad ones.

When teaching a puppy to fetch, start by getting the puppy excited about the fetch toy. Play with the toy and make a game of it.

The first few tosses should be short. A puppy's attention span is short and the dog may forget to come back. Continue calling to keep the dog moving in the right direction.

Good habits include: Waiting until the "Fetch" command is given to break for the dummy; running right to the dummy, picking it up and running right back to you; holding the dummy until you take it; giving up the dummy on command.

Anything else is a bad habit. Do not allow it. So, here are some tips for creating these good habits.

Steadiness: Give the "Sit" command before each toss. If the dog breaks after the throw but before the "Fetch" command, call her back (or pull on the long check cord) and give the command again. Wait five seconds. Point to the dummy and say, "Fetch." Two things are really important here. Don't be too firm in commanding the dog, especially a young dog, if it breaks with the throw. Remember, this is supposed to be fun. But also don't let the puppy get away with running to the dummy until you command it. Then, don't wait too long before giving the "Fetch" command. Young dogs might forget you tossed the dummy. As the dog gets older you can wait longer and longer to send the animal. For now, keep the wait just long enough to let the dog know you are in command.

Another way to steady the dog is to command, "Sit," toss the dummy and go get it yourself. Don't let the dog get up, reinforce the command if you need to and pick up the dummy and toss it again. Then say, "Fetch."

Straight there and straight back: On these early tosses, straight there should be no problem. If it is a problem, shorten up the toss even more, point

These training sessions give you the perfect opportunity to build on other blocks in the training foundation. Don't hesitate to repeat some of the previous commands you feel you have mastered.

Notice there are no sticks in this pile of fetch toys. Sticks are accidents waiting to happen. Buy good fetch toys.

to the dummy and say, "Fetch." Straight, back should just be your dog's response to the "Come" command. If the dog runs off, go get him and run the drill on a long lead so you can reel him in.

Holding the dummy: If the dog picks up the dummy and drops it, you have some work to do. Get the dog at heel standing next to you. Hold the dummy in your hand and say, "Fetch." Then put the dummy into the dog's mouth. If he drops it, say, "No. Fetch," and put the dummy back in the dog's mouth. Then, wait five seconds and say, "Give" and take the dummy. Slowly work up to longer and longer times that you require the dog to hold the dummy. After several training sessions, your dog should hold that dummy as long as you can stand to wait, then release it precisely on command. When the dog has that mastered, toss the dummy, say, "Fetch" and see what happens.

During all of this training session, I have quietly stressed pointing at the dummy as you give the command to "Fetch." The dog will see you pointing now and always find something fun (in this case, the dummy) in the direction you are pointing. It won't take long for a young dog to figure out that by heading in the direction you point he will find something he likes. And when he brings it back and gets that pat on the head, he'll feel like he just won the lottery. A dog that works happily should be your ultimate goal.

The Flying Squirrel is a great fetch toy that will provide hours of fun.

All of these training sessions give you the perfect opportunity to build on the other blocks in the training foundation. During these early retrieval sessions, don't hesitate to spring some of the other commands on the dog, or to stop tossing the dummy to work on the previous commands you feel you have mastered. Keep your whistle with you for every training session and be consistent. By really training the dog for 15 minutes and playing with the animal for another 5 to 15 minutes, you will build your puppy's skills, and you will create strong, permanent bonds with your pet.

Other fun fetch games

If you don't have a dummy and don't want to get one, a tennis ball makes a pretty good substitute. And there are some games you can play with a tennis ball that just don't work with a retrieval dummy. The bouncing ball is one of them. Try bouncing a dummy and you won't have much fun at all, but with a tennis ball you can get your dog all stirred up and excited, then whip the ball hard right at the ground and say "Sit" as the ball bounces skyward. As it comes down for the first bounce, give the "Fetch" command. With some dogs, catching the bouncing ball can be a great test of agility—and it's really fun to watch.

Throwing a Frisbee for a dog was popularized a couple decades ago when a few nimble dogs were seen making acrobatic catches during the halftime shows at football games. It's true that you can train a dog to accomplish such feats, but the reality is that it takes an impressive combination of training, athleticism and skill to pull this off. In short you need the right kind of dog, good training and you need to learn to throw the disk just about perfectly. I personally have never owned a dog with that kind of leaping ability (unless he was trying to scale a kennel fence). And I've never been able to throw a Frisbee that well.

Swimming lessons take patience. Letting the pup splash in the shallows is a great way to build confidence around the water.

Now that's not to say I haven't had fun throwing one for the dog. It just seems that I've never been able make the connection that gets me on the highlight films. Most of the time, my dogs run alongside the flying disk until it lands and scratch at it on the ground until they can pick it up and bring it back. The whole process is carried out much the same way I would train the dog to retrieve a dummy, except that I give the "Fetch" command while the Frisbee is still flying.

Water retrieves

The first time you try to get your puppy into the water you might want to make sure that you either have your swimming suit on or that the thing you're about to throw is something you don't mind losing.

Some dogs take to water like fish. Others need to be convinced that water is fun. It's not a difficult task...most of the time...but there are some instances that can be challenging.

The one thing you don't want to do is rush a dog that shows any hesitation about going into the water. If you pick up your dog and drop him off a dock, you could end up with an animal that suffers from a severe phobia. So take it slowly. Start at the water's edge with your dog's favorite fetch toy and you in your swimming suit.

The first thing to do is take the dog's mind off the water. Do this by teasing the dog with the dummy, getting the animal all excited, then tossing the dummy right on the edge of the water. The goal is to place the dummy in the water, but so close the dog can reach it without getting too wet. As soon as the dog grabs the dummy, lavish the animal with praise. Then do it again and again, making tosses into deeper water so the dog has to wade out a bit to get the dummy. Once the dog is confident charging into water up to her belly, it's time for you to get wet.

Puppies tire quickly on warm days. Keep the play sessions short, and provide plenty of water afterward.

Wade out into knee-deep water while teasing the dog with the dummy. Make your first toss parallel to shore and excitedly encourage the dog to go for the dummy. As the dog goes into the water you walk to shore to receive the dummy. Keep tossing deeper and deeper until the dog is swimming for the dummy. At this point, you're about done. All you have to do is keep making longer and longer throws into the deep water. The dog will figure out what to do.

Don't overdo it

Fetch is a game that most dogs will love, but you can get too much of a good thing. As I said at the beginning, law enforcement agencies look for dogs that willingly will fetch until your arm is tired. This means not all dogs will do this. Too much of the game, especially on hot days or with long water retrieves, can tire a dog to the point that she will not go on. Don't run your dog to the point of exhaustion because once he lies down and realizes that he doesn't really have to fetch things for you, it might be the end of the game, permanently. Keep the sessions to about 10 or 15 minutes, and then break up the activity with some other sort of play. You can go back to fetching things later, but don't overdo it during one session. Remember, it's a game. It's supposed to be fun.

Other Training Tips: Chewing can be solved

Sooner or later, you'll have to deal with a puppy that's chewed something to pieces. The first thing you have to know is that scolding your puppy after it has misbehaved is fruitless. If you catch the puppy in the act of chewing, remove the object and issue a correction with a very firm "No." Let the puppy sense, through the firmness of your voice, that chewing is unacceptable. Correct your puppy quietly and firmly each time you catch him chewing. You should also remember that chewing is natural behavior for a puppy. It eases the discomfort of teething, and is part of how the puppy explores his environment—through the sense of taste. Boredom may also lead to chewing; be certain your puppy gets plenty of time to play and enjoys walks with family members. Before leaving your puppy alone, take him for a walk or spend time playing with him. He will have less energy for chewing. Then you have to make sure that he doesn't have anything to chew. Confine the puppy to his crate and use the old trick of keeping the pup in the crate while your are out of sight, but in a location where the puppy can still hear you. This eases the puppy into an understanding that being alone is nothing to be afraid of.

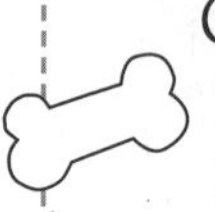

Chewing is part of the "puppy experience." You can't avoid it, but you can control it. Harsh discipline will be counterproductive.

PHOTO BY JULIA JOHNSON

Puppies don't realize that some things shouldn't be chewed. Firmly correct this behavior, replace the shoe with an appropriate chew toy, then praise the new activity.

If you feel like you must give your puppy some outlet for the chewing, don't give her anything that resembles anything you want to protect. Puppies cannot tell the difference between the toy and the real thing. Give your puppy safe chew toys, such as rawhide bones and hard rubber toys. Avoid toys containing parts that might come loose and be swallowed, such as plastic eyes or metal balls. To encourage the proper behavior, praise him when he plays with his chew toys. Get down there and play along. Make it enjoyable.

If you want to stop the puppy from chewing things he's not supposed to chew, treat them with hot pepper or with Bitter Apple, a bad-tasting (but safe) product available at pet stores. It won't take long for the young dog to figure out that chewing on items so treated is not fun.

Try to always keep in mind that chewing is part of the "puppy experience." In most cases, you can't avoid it, but you can control it. Harsh discipline will be counterproductive. A better strategy is to take steps to keep the pup away from the things that might be chewed.

Jumping causes trouble

There is nothing more loveable than a playful pup trying to reach up to get attention and playtime. It's cute, it makes people smile…and it must be stopped immediately! I'm not an ogre; I'm just thinking long-term. Puppies that jump become dogs that jump. Puppies get bigger. So (depending on breed of course), if you have a puppy that jumps, sooner or later you will likely have a big dog that jumps. Nothing turns people off more than a dog jumping all over the place. As cute and loveable as it is to have a happy little puppy jumping up and trying to get your attention, you have to put a stop to it. Luckily, it's pretty easy.

Maintaining calm around your pup will prevent some jumping, but when it happens be ready to act with firm, but gentle correction. They will soon get the message.

The first thing you have to do is pay attention to your actions. If you want a calm puppy, be a calm handler. The puppy will get as excited as you get. If you use a high, squeaky doggie voice and start roughhousing, expect an active response from your dog. That's fine. Go ahead. Do it. But when the puppy jumps, put your hand right in its face and issue a firm "No" command. Then, make the pup sit while you count slowly to 10. This gives you both a chance to calm down. On puppies, the firm voice command works just about every time. But if you are in a position that doesn't allow you get a hand in the pup's face—say sitting down in the grass or something — get one hand beneath the forelegs on the chest and quick but gently flip the puppy backwards as you say, "No!"

The little flip looks a lot more traumatic than it really is, but as with all dog training, the key is control. Don't use more force than you need. The flip works a lot like using a gentle knee in the chest for adult dogs that jump. Timing is everything, so you don't really want the pup to see what you have done. The correction comes because the dog—or in this case the puppy—thinks that jumping up caused the little back flip. That tumble, along with your voice command should make the pup think, "I don't want to try that again."

Keeping a puppy off furniture is another story entirely. This is where the old saying about an ounce of prevention being worth a pound of cure comes in really handy. If you don't invite your pet up on the furniture, you can avoid this problem completely. But, you'll still have to deal with that cute little puppy looking up at you with those sad eyes just begging to be invited up.

PHOTO BY JULIA JOHNSON

Curiosity in strange environments is good, but keeping your puppy leashed will help you quickly put a stop to aggressive behavior.

Now, I'm not telling you what to do, but understand this: Once that puppy is allowed up on the furniture, breaking the habit will be damned near impossible. If, on the other hand, you issue a firm verbal correction when the puppy tries to climb up with you on a chair or couch, the young dog will know its place. If you welcome the dog up, even once, it will also know its place. So, to use a Pavlovian cliché, you can't un-ring the bell. Once the puppy is up there, it's there for good.

Interrupt the aggression

Aggressive behavior, either towards humans or other pets, can no more be tolerated than can jumping up on strangers and little children. Luckily, starting with a puppy means you won't be trying to break any bad habits. From the moment you get your puppy, treat the animal fairly but firmly. Do anything you can to show that you are in control and the puppy is at all times subservient to humans. Now, I know that sounds rather draconian, but it's just a fact of life. Dogs have had eons "training," learning to live by the law of the pack. Simply put, the leader of the pack makes the rules, and if anyone challenges the leader there will be some sort of a struggle for supremacy. The dominant animal will prevail. In the wild, the leader—the alpha dog, if you will—eats first, gets the best resting places and initiates playtime or any other activities. Sounds a lot like what you as a dog owner will now be doing, doesn't it? Assume that responsibility and take control. The best thing you can do to show the puppy that you are boss is to control its food. Fill the bowl, place it on the floor and restrain the puppy. Then, when the puppy is eating, put your hands in the bowl and play with the food (this works much better with dry kibble). If the puppy shows any aggression, issue a firm reprimand and grab the puppy by the scruff of the neck and pull him away from the food. Only let him eat when you say it is time to eat.

The same is true during socialization (see the next page). When you are out and about, keep the puppy on a leash and watch for any aggressive behavior. There's a difference between bold and aggressive. A curious puppy that's willing to look around and explore is just fine. But put a stop to any baring of the teeth and growling right away with a quick tug on the leash and a stern verbal warning. Then, pick the puppy up and take him to investigate the cause of his concern. All the while use a soothing voice to show that aggression is not the way to deal with the issue. Again, because we are dealing with puppies, the issue is more about prevention than remedial training. If you don't allow the puppy to be aggressive, the animal will not be aggressive. If you allow or—worse yet—encourage the behavior, you'll have serious issues when the dog is full grown.

The more loving interaction you establish now, the stronger the bond your dog will have with you later.

Socialization

What your puppy learns about people and his environment now will stay with him for the rest of his life. From his fourth to his twelfth week, a puppy acquires almost all of his adult sensory, motor and learning abilities. The more loving interaction you establish now, the stronger the bond your dog will have with you later. Plan to spend at least two periods per day playing with your puppy. Use playtime to teach your puppy the basic training commands.

As soon as your veterinarian says it's safe, you should also begin exposing your puppy to as much of the outside world as possible. Introduce your pup to a variety of positive experiences. Visit three new places each week and introduce him to five new people at each place (find a variety of people). Take your pup on regular car rides—use a carrier to ensure safer driving.

Puppies may be predisposed to developing phobias between 8 and 11 weeks of age. During this time, you may want to be cautious when exposing your puppy to particularly stressful experiences, like large crowds and unusually loud noises. If your puppy becomes frightened, reassure him in a cheerful voice and pass it off quickly. Keep in mind that your puppy will sense feelings from you, so keep your response fairly matter-of-fact. Too much attention to a frightening experience may actually encourage a phobia.

Brush your pup daily, offering affection and reassurance to make it a special time for both of you. Also, handle your puppy's feet and ears and open his mouth for inspection. Massage him all over. If the pup fusses, say "No" firmly. When he is quiet, talk to him in a soft, pleasant voice. Similarly, teaching your puppy to allow you to wipe his paws now will be a real asset when he's full grown, bounding inside with wet feet on a rainy day!

Puppies need playmates, but first make sure the young dog is socialized to the idea that humans are in control.

Chapter Nine

Your Puppy's Health

During the nursing period, a puppy receives protective antibodies from its mother's milk. This natural immunity will begin to disappear with time, and may be gone soon after weaning. Consequently, around 8 to 10 weeks of age, a puppy is susceptible to a number of diseases. That's why it is so vital to take your puppy to a veterinarian as soon as possible for a check-up and vaccinations. Even if you have worked with the best, most reputable breeder in the nation, puppies hang around where germs live and sooner or later one of those germs will attack the little guy.

Your veterinarian can assess the general health of your puppy and point out any problems. If you buy your puppy from a breeder, the breeder may have given the puppy his first vaccination, but don't count on it. Ask. Get a detailed list of what medicines the breeder has given to the puppy and take that list to your veterinarian. As with human healthcare, good record keeping will insure things go smoothly.

All puppies should be vaccinated against canine diseases, checked periodically for worms and other parasites, and given an annual medical examination. Perhaps the most responsible thing you can do for your pet is to see that he receives timely health care from a veterinarian. His life depends on it. I will not try to substitute for a trained canine health care professional here and I don't advocate self-diagnosis. When compared to the cost of your puppy and the costs of your puppy's routine care, veterinary care is a bargain. Figure in the personal factors and for many people canine care becomes mandatory. This chapter is intentionally brief, with only an overview of a few symptoms and a reminder of required care. If your dog has a problem, or you even suspect a problem, get your dog to a vet. Early diagnosis can save a lot future problems.

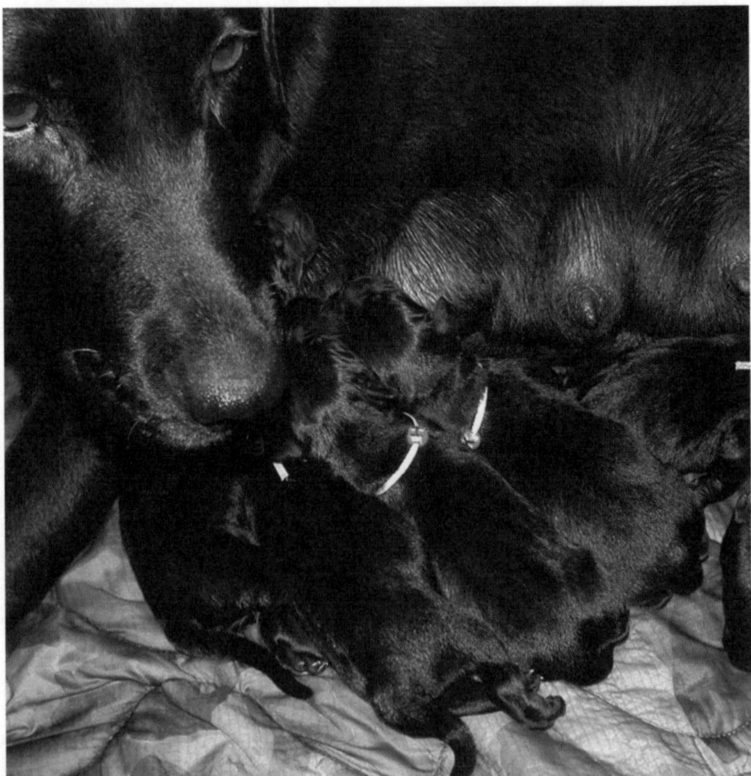

PHOTO BY JULIA JOHNSON

Puppies received natural antibodies through their mother's milk. But, this protection from disease starts to fade after weaning, and it will be up to you and your veterinarian to protect your puppy's health.

All puppies should be vaccinated against canine diseases, checked periodically for worms and other parasites, and given an annual medical examination.

Vaccinations

All puppies need to be vaccinated against disease according to the schedule provided by your veterinarian.

Your veterinarian may provide routine vaccinations for canine distemper, infectious canine hepatitis, leptospirosis, parvovirus, coronavirus, parainfluenza, Bordetella, Lyme disease and rabies. Remember, most vaccines must be given over a period of time and require multiple veterinary visits. So check with your veterinarian and make regular appointments for your young dog. If you don't, you can have some of the following diseases to deal with:

Distemper

A highly contagious, often-fatal virus that affects a dog's respiratory, gastrointestinal and nervous systems. Generally, this virus spreads as an airborne infection, so vaccination is the only effective control.

PHOTO BY JULIA JOHNSON

Closely monitor your new puppy. If you see any changes in his behavior, or early signs of illness, call your veterinarian.

Adenovirus (also know as infection hepatitis)

A viral disease that affects the liver and cells lining the blood vessels, causing high fever, thirst, loss of appetite, abdominal pain, liver damage, and hemorrhage.

Coronavirus

A highly contagious viral infection of the gastrointestinal tract. Symptoms include vomiting, diarrhea, high fever and dehydration.

Leptospirosis

An extremely contagious disease that spreads through contact with nasal secretions, urine or saliva of infected animals. It can affect humans as well. The ailment causes inflamed kidneys, fever, vomiting and diarrhea. Liver damage can also occur.

Parinfluenza (Bordetella)

This virus is one of a number of infectious agents that cause what is often called "kennel cough." The disease is highly contagious and attacks the respiratory system.

Parvovirus

A common and deadly viral infection whose symptoms include diarrhea, fever and vomiting. Parvovirus can kill puppies very quickly.

Rabies

A fatal infection of the central nervous system that affects all mammals, especially raccoons, bats, skunks, foxes, domestic dogs and cats, and humans. Since rabies poses a serious public health threat, it is imperative that your puppy be vaccinated. Most states require it.

Every veterinarian should be able to handle the wide range of medications your puppy will need. And visits to the vet are perfect times to ask general health and care questions about your dog. If there is something you need to know, chances are very good your veterinarian will have the answer. Getting to know your veterinarian is the beginning of a very beneficial relationship.

Monitoring your pet's health

How well do you know your pet? Because our pets cannot tell us how they feel, they may become quite ill before signs of their illness become apparent to us. Being aware of their usual behavior and appearance enables us to observe signs of illness and seek veterinary care before a condition worsens.

Back in Chapter 3, Dr. Arleigh Reynolds from Purina advised us to weigh puppies regularly and to make sure they are not growing too quickly. This is all part of the monitoring process. When you take on the responsibility of a new puppy, you also become the first line of defense when it comes to illness and medical care. As it is with humans, early diagnosis is sometimes the key to a successful cure. The more attention you pay, the better chance you'll have to catch something early.

Healthy dogs combine contentment and alertness. They usually stretch on rising, look relaxed when resting and respond to activities around them. A trip to the vet is in order if you observe:

Loss of appetite: Dogs occasionally to go "off feed" for a day or two, but if appetite loss persists consult your vet.

Lameness: Any time a puppy shows problems walking, have the dog checked right away. It could be the first signs of something very serious.

Blood in the urine: You'll need to pay attention on trips outside. It's not pleasant, but it is important.

Haircoat with harsh feel or dull texture: This can be caused by a food problem or trouble in the digestive system.

Mucus or blood visible in the stools: Again, not pleasant, but important. If you clean up regularly, you will notice this right away.

Foul-smelling stools: Worse than normal.

Repeated vomiting over several days: This is the sign of something serious and also leads to dehydration.

Potbelly or loss of weight: It's easy to spot.

This puppy appears to be the picture of health, but don't take unnecessary chances. Regular check-ups, along with the recommended vaccinations, will ensure that your dog is healthy and happy.

Chewing on toys is okay, but if your puppy starts to chew on its feet or skin, it can be a sign of parasites, allergies, or even a more serious illness.

"Bloated" or distended belly that's firm to touch: Also easy to spot. Get this checked right away.

Lack of interest in what is happening: This can be something minor or a sign of serious issues, so don't let it pass unnoticed.

Hiding in dark places: Never a good thing.

Persistent coughing; discharge from the eyes and nose: Respiratory infections can take dogs quickly.

Scratching or chewing at feet, skin or haircoat: Usually parasites, but sometimes something worse.

Shaking head, scratching ears: Ear problems should never be left unattended.

Yellowing of the white around the eye, or yellow gums: Signs of a serious problem; a trip to the veterinarian is warranted.

Another sign of illness is dehydration, a deficit of water in a dog's body that can be life-threatening. To test for dehydration, pick up a fold of skin in the middle back area and then release it. Normally the skin will snap back. If it falls back slowly or remains up, dehydration is present. Immediate veterinarian care is needed to find the underlying cause and to administer fluids, either intravenously (in the blood vessels) or subcutaneously (under the skin), depending upon the degree of dehydration. Among the causes of extreme water loss are diarrhea, vomiting and excessive urination associated with diabetes, heart and renal disease.

Keeping a medical record of your pet's vaccinations, illnesses, injuries, surgeries or medication will be helpful when an emergency situation arises and your regular veterinarian is not available. If you move to another state, ask your current veterinarian for your pet's medical record to give to the veterinarian you select in your new location.

Two things to watch for:

Worms: Each time you take your dog into the vet for a routine check-up or for vaccinations, take a stool sample along and have the vet check for worms. These intestinal parasites come in many shapes and sizes, all of which can be harmful to your dog. They are easy to take care of once found, but you have to be on the lookout for them. The best way to avoid worms is to keep your dog's living areas clean, and to keep an eye on what the dog eats. Dogs living outside in a kennel might take stool into their mouths if the kennel is not kept clean. Aside from being really gross, that causes lots of health issues. Keep the kennels clean.

Fleas and ticks: Each time you play with and pet your puppy, make a cursory inspection for fleas and ticks. Check the head and behind the ears with your fingers, or a small comb or brush. Fleas appear like small flakes of pepper and show up on light-colored dogs easier than on dark dogs. If you see your dog scratching or gnawing at its sides, take a close look for fleas. As for ticks, you'll likely find them borrowed into the skin. Use a tweezers to grasp the tick as close to the skin as possible and pull it out with firm, steady pressure. Dab on some antibiotic ointment and you are ready to go.

Other medical care

As with anything in life there are two ways to look at medical care for your dog. You can opt to be remedial or you can choose to be preventative. The latter is better and will help keep your vet bills lower and you dog healthier. Sure, there will be times when you need to take immediate emergency action, but if you have established a good schedule of check-ups, your vet will

Active puppies that spend a lot of time outdoors are exposed to fleas and ticks. Carefully inspect their coats after playtime to make sure no unwanted guests hopped on your pet.

If you have an active dog and you get outside a lot, sooner or later you'll need to deal with minor injuries.

be familiar with your dog and you'll be familiar with the vet. It just makes things easier.

When talking about preventative medical care, don't overlook shots. Each municipality is likely to have different requirements, but all will require that your dog be vaccinated against rabies and distemper. Ask your vet to put you on a regular schedule; most will mail you a postcard when it's time for shots. Follow the schedule faithfully and ask a lot of questions. Is there anything else your dog needs to be vaccinated against? What about Lyme disease? Or kennel cough? Be informed; get your dog everything it needs.

Another concern is heartworm. Any place there are mosquitoes, your dog is exposed to potentially fatal heartworm infection. Until recently, veterinarians would prescribe heartworm medication only during the warm months of the year. Lately though, there has been a push for year-round defense against these deadly invaders. It only costs a little bit more to keep the dog on heartworm medicine year-round, so for the sake of your pet, buy the extra pills and administer them every month.

The long and short of preventive medicine is to get on your vet's mailing list and follow directions as they are given. I'm not telling you not to ask questions, just don't skimp on regular care for your pet. These regular visits can also aid in early detection of other diseases.

Build a first-aid kit for your dog

If you have an active dog and you get outside a lot, sooner or later you'll need to deal with minor injuries or make an emergency trip to the vet. You need to be ready for just such an eventuality. People tend to look at me a little bit funny when I say that I maintain a doggie first-aid kit in addition to the human model I keep in my house. But why not have one? I can't think of a good reason to do without it.

Medical care for dogs is a bit different than tending to bumps, scrapes and cuts with a human first-aid kit. I've found two items most important in my canine first-aid kit: Vetrap and a pair of locking forceps. Vetrap is the brand name of a clingy, bandage material made by the 3M Company that is almost self-adhesive without being sticky like tape. It's just the stuff you need if your dog suffers a cut that's big enough to require a bandage. Clean out the wound, put some gauze over the cut, wrap with a couple layers of Vetrap and take the dog for an exam.

The locking forceps are necessary because I live and travel in porcupine country. One encounter with a porcupine proved the need for some forceps. Future encounters were no less stressful, but the tool really made my first-aid much easier.

Your Canine First-Aid Kit

- Vetrap or a roll of gauze
- First-aid tape
- Sterile saline
- Gauze pads (3x3 inches or larger)
- Triple antibiotic ointment
- Lightweight muzzle
- Locking forceps
- Bandage scissors

Other items included in the doggie first-aid kit are sterile saline solution to be used as eyewash or to irrigate cuts before bandaging, gauze pads, triple antibiotic ointment and a lightweight muzzle. In only one instance did I not have a dog try to bite me as I administered medical care, and that dog had so many porcupine quills in his tongue, lips and nose that he seemed to know I was just there to help him.

If your dog gets hurt, the first thing you need to do is get control of him. Snap on the leash and, just as a precaution, put on the muzzle. The next step is to get some help. Most dogs don't like to sit still when they are hurt. You'll need at least one person to restrain and attempt to calm the dog while you get to work. Once you have the initial problem solved, get the dog to a veterinarian to make sure everything is fine.

PHOTO BY JULIA JOHNSON

It's important to keep your pet active, but remember that playtime accidents happen. Keep a first-aid kit handy for emergencies.

Chapter Ten

Having a Happy Dog

Bringing a puppy into your family is the only way to learn about living with, and training, a puppy. What you get from this book, or any book, is theory. Sure, these are tested methods that have worked well for others, and me, but the way you take care of your puppy will tell a lot about you.

Good training means you can trust your dog anywhere.

The first and most important thing you need to remember is this: Your puppy depends on you for *everything*.

That's just seven words, but they are quite complex—especially that last word. Think about it, your puppy needs you for everything. From food, water and shelter to medical care, training and exercise and right down to things like bathroom privileges and entertainment, your dog is dependent on you. There's no denying that, no way to get around the facts and once you have a dog, there's nothing you can do to change that, short of getting rid of the animal. And even then, if you choose to get rid of your dog, that animal is counting on you to find it a good home where it will be provided all the things you couldn't give.

So, when people say owning a dog is a big responsibility, they are correct. It's not quite as big a responsibility as raising children, but it's close. This has been short primer on basic pet care. True, many of you will say, "I already knew that," but I believe it's important to issue timely reminders, especially for people who are busy with other aspects of life. Sometimes dogs become secondary. I make no judgment about that because I, too, have to find time to balance work, family life, home maintenance, car repairs and dog ownership responsibilities. But if you just remember why you got the dog in the first place, that knowledge often makes it a bit easier to do everything you need to do to keep your dog healthy. Do you remember why you got the dog? If you break it down to its most basic element, nine out of 10 people

Remember this: Your puppy depends on you for everything.

buy a dog so the animal can provide happiness. With that in mind, let's talk about keeping your dog happy and healthy. What does it really take?

Food

All puppies have to eat and most really love eating. You can make your puppy happy with a dish of food. But should it be any old food? First of all, your average dog will eat just about any food you put in front of him. But that doesn't mean the food will be nutritionally complete. The cheapest dog food you can buy is just that. It's usually nothing but a lot of filler, some corn meal and a binding agent to make it all stick together. As frugal as I am, I'll regularly spend extra on premium-quality dog food. There are a couple of good reasons for this, above and beyond the fact that better food is better for the dog. Good quality food makes your life easier in two ways: less poop and less shedding. It's true. Give your dog some bargain-basement dog food, measure the amount and serve up two cups a day. Then make a note of how many times your dog defecates. With a top-quality food, your dog will go once a day and you may actually end up feeding her less food because with more in each bite that she's able to digest, your dog won't need as much food to maintain her weight. The same is true of shedding. Good dog food means a healthier coat and less hair floating around your house and car.

So, go to your vet and see what food is sold there. Buy a small bag and see how your dog handles it. If you really need to spend less on dog food, read the ingredients carefully on the premium bag, then go to your local discount store and see which national brand most closely matched both the ingredients and the percentages of protein, fat, moisture and crude fiber. Buy that food and you should be doing pretty well for your dog.

Follow the recommendations on the bag concerning amounts you are feeding, but also pay attention how much exercise your dog gets and the animal's weight. You want to keep the dog's energy level up, but you also don't want to see your dog packing on the pounds. If your dog spends time outdoors in the winter, you'll want to supply a bit more food (but water is also of major importance—see below). If the animal is working as a doorstop or a footrest in an air-conditioned apartment, cut back on the food.

Feeding time can be a bit of a challenge. Puppies and dogs being housebroken need to get several small meals each day. You can get away with feeding healthy adult dogs one meal per day, but you may decide you want to set a meal schedule, especially if your dog is overweight. If your hound is a fatty, go with a couple of smaller meals each day; that will help to change the dog's metabolism and help the animal to burn up more of the food that's eaten.

Water

This is the key element in your puppy's diet. Once the animal is housebroken there is not much need to restrict water. In some instances—such as periods of extreme temperatures—you'll want to insure that the dog has all the water it wants. Everyone knows dogs want water when it's hot. Dogs can't

> There is nothing more important to keeping a dog warm during the winter than ample water. The water helps the dog digest and metabolize the food it has eaten.

sweat, so they expel excess heat through their mouths by panting. With this heat goes a lot of moisture, meaning a dog can quickly dehydrate just by laying around panting.

On the other end of the spectrum is the water needed when a dog gets cold. There is nothing more important to keeping a dog warm during the winter than ample water. The water helps the dog digest and metabolize the food it has eaten. With no water, that interior furnace shuts down and even a dog with a belly full of food will get cold. I have dogs that live outside all year and the first thing I buy with a new dog is an electrically heated water bucket. For years I was chipping ice and providing fresh water about four times a day during the winter months. The electric bucket means I only need to refresh the water once a day and it will never be frozen.

While it's true that a thirsty dog will drink just about anything, your dog shouldn't have to. Make sure you keep the water dish clean and filled with fresh water. Keeping the dish clean means you have to wash it once in a while. Use a good quality cleaner to clean and disinfect the bowl at least twice a month; once a week is better. Keeping the bowl filled with fresh water means just that. Dogs have trouble drinking from shallow dishes. Have you ever watched a dog closely as he laps up water? The dog's tongue curls under toward his lower jaw and he pulls a bit of water up into his mouth. It's not very efficient and it's even less efficient from very shallow water bowls. So, make it easy for your dog with a dish that big enough, clean and filled with fresh water.

Shelter

"In the dog house" should not be a negative term. Your dog needs a place to call his own and you can make such a place as splendid or austere as you like, as long as you make it comfortable.

There are two kinds of dogs in the world: inside dogs and outside dogs. Outside dogs need different things than inside dogs, but they don't automatically need more things. If you plan to keep your dog outside (and that's perfectly acceptable) the best thing you can do is provide a kennel with some room to roam. Most home centers sell complete chain-link kennels in various sizes for less than $200. Buy a kennel that is 6 feet tall. Even if you have a relatively small dog, the 4-foot kennel means you'll be ducking and banging your head every time you go in and out. A kennel that is 12 feet long, 6 feet wide and 6 feet tall is fine for just about any dog. You can use compacted gravel, concrete patio blocks or poured concrete for the floor—just make sure it is something you can clean easily.

Inside the kennel, you'll want an insulated doghouse that's equipped with a wind-proof door and provides easy access for cleaning. There are plenty of injection-molded plastic models available. Or, if you are handy, the same home center that sold you the kennel will be happy to sell you a doghouse kit, a set of plans or lumber to allow you to build a house in any style you want.

If you plan to equip your kennel with an electrically heated water bucket (something I really suggest) you'll need to get a piece of conduit to shield the electric cord, just in case your dog gets bored and decides to chew something beside the dog house. Wire the conduit along the outside of one of the vertical support poles allowing only enough electric cord exposed to plug in the heated bucket.

For any kennel, make sure you have a secure latch. A lockable secure latch is even better. The lock not only insures the dog will not be able to flip the latch, but also provides some added security should anyone decide you have a really great dog.

As for inside dogs, just about anything goes. But one thing you need to provide is a portable kennel in an out-of-the-way place where the dog can go to avoid the noise and pace of an active household. Equip the portable

PHOTO BY JULIA JOHNSON

A roomy chain link kennel—available as a kit at many home centers—offers a safe and comfortable home for dogs living outside.

kennel with a good-quality doggie bed and set a schedule to keep the bed clean regularly.

Depending on your personal preferences, your housedog can have as many or as few restrictions as you see fit. Just remember to be consistent. Early in my marriage, my wife and I owned a happy little Cocker Spaniel (is there any other kind?). At first there was a strict rule against allowing the dog on any furniture, especially the bed. After my first business trip, the dog looked at me like I was insane when I ordered her off the bed. From that day forward the dog staked her claim on any piece of furniture that happened to rest in a warm or sunny spot.

Housedogs need food and water, like any other dog, but they also need protection from household products that can cause harm or even be fatal. If your dog has the run of the house, be sure to keep things like household cleaners, chemicals and other products secured in a cabinet or a room that is off limits to the dog.

Exercise

A dog might not always get enough exercise from your training sessions. Plan to include walks, runs and swimming in your scheduled outings. But do it wisely. Walking and running can be hard on a dog's feet. If you have a housedog and suddenly decide that it's time she becomes a little more active, don't just snap on the leash and take off on an hour walk around town. It will take a series of short trips to help the dog's muscles get used to the exercise, but more importantly it will take time to toughen up the pads on a dog's feet. Even hard-working dogs will get sore feet. A housedog used to a life of leisure will have soft pads and you'll often see the dog licking his feet after a long walk. Don't stop exercising because of this; just shorten up the trips for a while until the dog's feet get in shape.

Swimming falls into the same category. Not all dogs are born as strong swimmers. If you throw a ball or a dummy 10 yards into the water 10 times that means your dog is going to swim 200 yards. That's a lot of exercise. Don't overdo it.

If you run or jog and you want to take your dog with you, you don't have to worry so much about how far and fast you run, but you do need to think about your route. Are you running on gravel trails, sidewalks, along busy streets or up and down steep hills? Will you have your dog on a leash or will you require the animal to trot at your side? Do you need to carry water for your dog? Are there other dogs along the way? Are you able and willing to stop and scoop poop in the middle of your run?

You won't be totally building your workout around the dog, but you will be changing it to accommodate the fact that a dog is coming along with you. As every person and every dog is different, you'll need to experiment and tailor the route and the workout to what works for both you and the dog. It might be a good idea to carry a fanny pack with some water, a leash and perhaps a muzzle. Plan for the unexpected.

As with any exercise program, once you get started you need to keep your

Swimming is great exercise for dogs. The water will offer a new experience for your pup, but don't overdo it the first time out.

dog involved. These exercise trips become part of your dog's routine. If they are suddenly abandoned you could end up with a dog that needs to release extra energy—possibly by barking all day or chewing your furniture.

Entertainment

Let's face it, dogs are here for our entertainment. They are fun to play with and we enjoy having them around—but they are not toys. I often need to remind people, especially those with young children, that dogs get tired, bored and sometimes just want to be left alone. Dogs can have *too much* fun. That's why it's important to give them a safe and secure place to get away from it all. But even more important than that is to be able to recognize when the dog wants to be alone and to respond accordingly. That could mean telling your nieces and nephews to, "Leave Buffy alone for a while."

If you're planning a big gathering, or even a small one, involving people your dog is not familiar with, make sure the animal has ready access to an "escape route" that is off limits to your human guests, especially children. You don't have to have a "pre-party huddle" or post a list of doggie rules, but take some time to let people know what's going on as it becomes appropriate.

Some events that require special attention include any gathering that involves dancing and loud music, active outdoor games like volleyball, softball or soccer and groups of people who like to get loud and laugh a lot. You can invite the dog into these groups, but watch the animal's body language. If the dog is cowering or growling, get that animal back into

When raised together, kids and dogs get along very well. Teach both how to behave.

the portable kennel. Also, if the games are going on outside and the dog is running around looking confused, try to get him out of the melee. Place a favorite chew toy in the kennel and secure the door. Just remember to go back and check on the dog every once in a while, because this type of activity can upset the dog's regular rhythms concerning breaks to relieve itself. If the dog seems stressed and agitated while in the kennel, take a few minutes to let the dog out (on the leash of course) before you return to the party.

Also, if your dog is not used to having children around, don't subject the animal to the happy hands of the little ones. Kids are great, but they are tough on dogs. And, the younger the kid, the tougher it is for the dog to put up with the little guy's "playing." You never want to leave your dog in a situation where continued poking, prodding and playing could result in a youngster getting bit. It gives the dog an often-undeserved bad reputation and can cost you (or your home owners' insurance carrier) some serious cash.

It's best to keep kids and dogs closely monitored and to give the children direct instructions concerning the dog. You'll very likely want to encourage a good relationship between the youngster and the dog and the best way to do that is to control the child every bit as much as you control the dog.

One of the best things you can do for kids and dogs is to sit down with them and soothe the dog while you explain things and answer the child's questions. Show the youngster how the dog likes to be petted and point out that the dog's ears, eyes and nose are sensitive. Tell the child that if the dog gets up to walk away, that means he's done playing and wants to be left alone. Never let a child follow a dog that's trying to move away. The dog only wants to create some space and be left alone. An overly persistent youngster might just make the dog angry. Step in and stop that before it gets out of hand.

Finally, people have written entire books on basic dog care, but the truth is they are all about opinion. If you look long enough you can find a book that supports your ideas of how you should take care of your new puppy. Don't ever discount your beliefs or God-given common sense. If you are providing food, water, shelter and basic but effective training, you are on the right track to having a healthy and happy dog. The only other thing you need to concentrate on is kindness. Think of your puppy as your friend. Provide your training, even your corrections, consistently. Be kind and patient, but persistent, and your dog will respond to your training quickly and will remain happy and well adjusted. If you think something you're doing isn't quite right, go with your gut. If you still have questions, ask your veterinarian. Most of the time you'll find out you were right all along and you just needed that affirmation to prove that you were on the right track.

Puppy training doesn't have to be difficult and dog care doesn't have to be demanding. You can have a great puppy with just 15 minutes a day for your training and little bit of extra time for fun. If you follow that basic schedule, you'll see that dog ownership provides more benefits than you could have imagined.

PHOTO BY JULIA JOHNSON

With the right mix of training and kindness, your puppy can become a great friend, ready to share many of life's adventures with you.

Appendix: Listing of AKC Breeds

This is the list of breeds currently recognized by the American Kennel Club. If you can't find a dog you like on this list, you might just be a cat person. There is something for everyone here. Check out www.AKC.org for information about helping you select a breed or breeder and find out more about the joys and responsibilities of owning a purebred puppy.

Affenpinscher
Afghan Hound
Airedale Terrier
Akita
Alaskan Malamute
American Eskimo Dog
American Foxhound
American Staffordshire Terrier
American Water Spaniel
Anatolian Shepherd Dog
Australian Cattle Dog
Australian Shepherd
Australian Terrier

B

Basenji
Basset Hound
Beagle
Bearded Collie
Bedlington Terrier
Belgian Malinois
Belgian Sheepdog
Belgian Tervuren
Bernese Mountain Dog
Bichon Frise
Black and Tan Coonhound
Black Russian Terrier
Bloodhound
Border Collie
Border Terrier
Borzoi
Boston Terrier
Bouvier des Flandres
Boxer
Briard
Brittany
Brussels Griffon
Bull Mastiff
Bull Terrier
Bulldog

C

Cairn Terrier
Canaan Dog
Cardigan Welsh Corgi
Cavalier King Charles Spaniel
Chesapeake Bay Retriever
Chihuahua
Chinese Crested
Chinese Shar-Pei
Chow Chow
Clumber Spaniel
Cocker Spaniel

Collie
Curly-Coated Retriever

D

Dachshund
Dalmatian
Dandie Dinmont Terrier
Doberman Pinscher

E

English Cocker Spaniel
English Foxhound
English Setter
English Springer Spaniel
English Toy Spaniel

F

Field Spaniel
Finnish Spitz
Flat-Coated Retriever
French Bulldog

G

German Pinscher
German Shepherd Dog
German Shorthaired Pointer
German Wirehaired Pointer
Giant Schnauzer
Golden Retriever
Gordon Setter
Great Dane
Great Pyrenees
Greater Swiss Mountain Dog
Greyhound

H

Harrier
Havanese

I

Ibizan Hound
Irish Setter
Irish Terrier
Irish Water Spaniel
Irish Wolfhound
Italian Greyhound

J

Japanese Chin

K

Keeshond
Kerry Blue Terrier
Komondor
Kuvasz

L

Labrador Retriever
Lakeland Terrier
Lhasa Apso
Löwchen

M

Maltese
Manchester Terrier
Mastiff
Miniature Bull Terrier
Miniature Pinscher
Miniature Schnauzer

N

Neapolitan Mastiff
Newfoundland
Norfolk Terrier
Norwegian Elkhound
Norwich Terrier
Nova Scotia Duck Tolling Retriever

O

Old English Sheepdog
Otterhound

P

Papillon
Parson Russell Terrier
Pekingese
Pembroke Welsh Corgi
Petit Basset Griffon Vendéen
Pharaoh Hound
Pointer
Polish Lowland Sheepdog
Pomeranian
Poodle
Portuguese Water Dog
Pug
Puli

R

Rhodesian Ridgeback
Rottweiler

S

Saluki
Samoyed
Schipperke
Scottish Deerhound
Scottish Terrier
Sealyham Terrier
Shetland Sheepdog
Shiba Inu
Shih Tzu
Siberian Husky
Silky Terrier
Skye Terrier
Smooth Fox Terrier
Soft Coated Wheaten Terrier
Spinone Italiano
St. Bernard
Staffordshire Bull Terrier
Standard Schnauzer
Sussex Spaniel

T

Tibetan Spaniel
Tibetan Terrier
Toy Fox Terrier

V

Vizsla

W

Weimaraner
Welsh Springer Spaniel
Welsh Terrier
West Highland White Terrier
Whippet
Wire Fox Terrier
Wirehaired Pointing Griffon

Y

Yorkshire Terrier

Bibliography and Resources

Books

American Kennel Club. *The Complete Dog Book, 19th Ed.* Howell Book House, 1998.
This is probably the most popular resource for studying up on, and comparing the traits of, the 146 AKC-recognized breeds.

Benjamin, Carol Lea. *The Chosen Puppy: How to Select and Raise a Great Puppy from an Animal Shelter*. Howell House Books, 1990.
A popular handbook for people who are planning to adopt a puppy from an animal shelter—a great place to get a great dog.

Boone, Eugene. *The Big Book of Pet Names*. RSVP Press, 2004.
More than 10,000 possible names for your puppy.

Coile, D. Caroline and Michele Earle-Bridges. *Barron's Encyclopedia of Dog Breeds.* Barron's Educational Series, 1998.
A colorful and comprehensive guide to AKC breeds—a good resource for selecting the right purebred dog.

Fogle, Bruce and Amanda Williams. *First Aid for Dogs: What to Do When Emergencies Happen*. Penguin Books, 1997.
A good addition to your dog's first-aid kit.

Garvey, Michael S. DVM, et al. *The Veterinarian's Guide to Your Dog's Symptoms.* Villard, 1999.
This is a concise book that uses a flow-chart system to help dog owners analyze 150 common symptoms.

Griffin, James M., and Liisa D. Carlson. *Dog Owner's Home Veterinary Handbook.* Howell Book House, 1999.
A comprehensive, highly illustrated, easy-to-use guide to every aspect of your dog's health.

Michalowski, Kevin. *15 Minutes to a Great Dog*. Krause Publications, 2002.
The author's companion volume focused on training older dogs.

Siegal, Mordecai. *UC Davis Book of Dogs: The Complete Medical Reference for Dogs and Puppies*. HarperResources, 1995.
A comprehensive guide to dog health, growth, development, feeding, and much more. Very good, but technical.

Storer, Pat. *Crate Training Your Dog*. Storey Books, 2000.
This 32-page booklet gives you quick and easy tips on house training dogs of all ages.

Internet Sites

www.aboutdogs.com

A website devoted to all things dogs, with several perspectives for each topic.

www.akc.org

The American Kennel Club web site. Focused on purebreds, but packed with all kinds of goodies for anybody that loves dogs.

www.dogchow.com

Great site, but with a decidedly Purina attitude. If you can ignore sales pitch you'll be fine.

www.drsfostersmith.com

The website of the world-famous Drs. Foster and Smith catalog—the best dogs beds and everything else you need, including advice.

www.dunns.com

A dog training supply house of the first order if you love hunting dogs and the sporting life. Nothing cheap here. This is all top-of-the-line stuff.

www.gooddogmagazine.com

Previously a print publication, now web-only. Primary focus is product test reports on dog foods and other dog products.

www.inch.com/~dogs/index.htm

The link to the American Dog Trainers Network. This site has everything. It will point you in the right direction, no matter what your question.

www.petcarerx.com

This site will give you good look at pet medications, including some tips on use and ailments, but always check with your local vet first.

www.petplace.com

This is a fee-based website that provides lots of information and articles from pet specialists of all types.

www.petrix.com/dognames

A simple site listing more than 2,000 possible names for your puppy.

www.thepetcenter.com

Bills itself as the Internet animal hospital. Lots of good information, but double check with a reputable vet.

www.workingdogs.com

An online "cyberzine" devoted to working and sporting dogs—sled dogs, herders, trackers, police dogs, search and rescue dogs and much more.

Index